GOODBYE BYLINE, HELLO BIG BUCKS

Make Money Ghostwriting Books, Articles, Blogs, and More

SECOND EDITION

Kelly James-Enger

IMPROVISE PRESS

Visit the Improvise Press Website: www.improvisepress.com

Printed in the United States of America

ISBN: 978-0-9888185-0-7

To Ryan and Haley, my favorite reasons to ghostwrite

TABLE OF CONTENTS

ACKNOWLEDGEMENTS

Writers spend most of our working lives alone. If we're lucky though, there's a whole team of people integral to our lives and our success—and I'm not just talking about the people who hire and pay us, though I'm very grateful to my past (and future) clients.

So I'd like to acknowledge the dozens of people—ghostwriters, coauthors, content marketing writers, ghost bloggers, literary agents, corporate historians, and publishing experts—who graciously shared their insights, experience, and advice to enrich this book. I'm especially grateful to: Jill Amadio, Kendra Bonnett, Kathi Ann Brown, Marian Calabro, Sharon Cindrich, Sondra Forsyth, Helen Gallagher, Claire Gerus, Stephanie Golden, Timothy Gower, Jennifer Goforth Gregory, Jodi Helmer, Kelly Kautz, Heidi Tyline King, Linda Konner, Jacquelyn Lynn, Gwen Moran, Randy Myers, Ellen Neuborne, Leah Nicholson, Jill Russell Qualizza, Fern Reiss, Ed Robertson, Erik Sherman, Graciela Sholander, Marcia Layton Turner, and Melanie Votaw.

This book also couldn't have happened without Keri and Diana, without whom I'd be unable to work (or even concentrate). I'm also very thankful for my in-house IT consultant, Erik, for all of the many roles he plays in my life, not the least of which is awesome spouse—and super-daddy to Ryan and Haley.

INTRODUCTION

You're not only a writer—you're a writer who writes for money. A freelancer. Someone who sells his words for pay.

So, let me ask you—how attached are you to your byline? How much does it matter to you?

Nearly every writer wants recognition. But ditching your byline may be the smartest thing you ever do for your writing career. The market for talented ghostwriters is huge, and continuing to grow. Household names like Hillary Rodham Clinton, David Beckham, Donald Trump, Naomi Campbell, and Clay Aiken are all authors who used ghostwriters. An estimated 80 percent of celebrity-authored books are ghostwritten, and publishing experts say that half of *The New York Times* bestsellers are ghosted, too.

But it's not just big names who hire ghostwriters and book collaborators; the market for writers who can pen someone else's book is broad and growing. Book publishers, literary agents, book packagers, corporations, and everyday people all pay ghostwriters to write their books.

And that's just books. Ghostwriters now craft everything from blog posts to articles to content marketing pieces to white papers and even Tweets. Corporations are spending more than 40 billion dollars every year on content marketing, and need writers to ghost that work.

If you're a freelancer who wants to branch into a growing, lucrative niche; a book author who wants to make more money in less time; or a writer who wants to be paid (and paid well) for your work, it's time to say, "goodbye" to your byline—and "hello!" to big bucks.

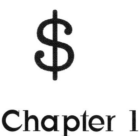

Chapter 1

Say Goodbye to Your Byline: Why Become a Ghostwriter?

I've always said that there are two kinds of writers. Those who want to write, and those who want to make money from their work.

Millions of us claim ourselves as writers, and give up free time to pen novels, short stories, memoirs, essays, and blog posts—not to mention clever Facebook statuses, and compelling, less-than-140-character Tweets. For these people, writing is a creative act, a compulsion, an enjoyable (at least sometimes) hobby.

I'm not one of those writers. Not anymore, anyway. My days of writing for nothing more than creative satisfaction (and possible praise, if I showed my work to anyone) came to end when I decided I wanted to quit my job as an attorney and write full-time. Now my creative urge had to be sublimated my business sense, my need to make money, and my drive to succeed as a self-employed writer.

That was more than 17 years ago, and things have changed in the freelancing field. A lot. When I started writing fulltime, there were at least a thousand print markets—consumer, trade, and custom magazines—that paid freelancers pretty well, say $1/word and up. There were promising online markets, too, with plenty of websites paying fair rates. Sure, some publishers had all-rights, or "work-for-hire" contracts, for articles, but the work-for-hires hadn't become the norm. I found it relatively easy to make a living writing articles for magazines, and cracked the six-figure market my fifth year of fulltime freelancing.

Well, things have changed—and many of those changes haven't been positive ones for freelancers. Print magazines have shrunk, and average assignments have gotten shorter. Yet per-word rates have remained the same; many magazines still start at $1/word, the same rate they paid in the 1960s. While rates haven't gone up, publishers now want more than ever before.

The all-rights contract has now becoming pro forma for big publishers. That means for a set amount of money, the publisher has the right to do whatever it wants with your piece—while you never see another penny from it.

In the meantime, "content mills" devalue writers' work, promising so-called "opportunities" for fledgling writers. With these sites, you can make $5—or even more—per article! (Please note my sarcasm.) The fact that so many newbies (clueless or not) are willing to write for next to nothing drives down the average pay rates and makes uninformed clients and editors think that they can get writing for nearly free. And they can. But good writing? Well-researched, compelling, accurate writing? Not so much.

Things have changed in the book world too. A decade and a half ago, if you wanted to become an author, you had two options—sell your book to a traditional publisher, or pay a vanity publisher to get your book in print. New authors had a decent chance of selling a book to a publishing house if they had a strong concept and a unique take on a subject. Advances for first-time authors of nonfiction hovered around the $10,000 range, but plenty of authors made much more than that.

Today? Traditional publishers care about one thing, and it's called platform, which encapsulates your ability to sell a book. If you don't have strong social media numbers (think tens of thousands of Twitter followers), you're going to have a hard time selling your book, even if the idea is unique and your writing, stellar. And if you do, expect that advance to be paltry—maybe just a few thousand dollars.

Of course you may opt to circumvent the traditional process altogether, and choose a print-on-demand company. Then you'll be paying to publish your book—instead of a publisher paying you. Despite that fact, POD companies are outpacing traditional publishers, and electronic books are the fastest growing segment of the market.

More people than ever before are making the transition from "wanting to publish a book" to "published author." That's great for them—not so great for authors who want to sell books as there's significantly more competition. Authors have to market more aggressively than ever before—and that marketing time means you have fewer hours in the day to actually make money.

But Wait—There Is Good News

Are you depressed yet? Don't be. It's actually a great time to be writing for money. Because while we may be overwhelmed by information (according to one study, we're exposed to the equivalent of 174 80-page newspapers' worth of data every day!), that information comes from somewhere. Corporations, publishers, nonprofits, and individuals must keep on producing content. They need content. And they need people—writers—to produce that content.

I use the word content for a reason. The fastest growing opportunity for freelancers is something called "content marketing," which nine out of ten companies use to promote their products and services." Content marketing is where the money is, yet most freelancers don't realize how lucrative this niche can be—or how to break into it.

If you're already freelancing, you know it takes more than writing ability to be successful. Whether you're writing an article for a trade magazine, a blog post for an entertainment website, or a case study for a corporate client, you have to communicate information while using a particular voice or tone—that of the market or client you're writing for. That skill is arguably the most important one you need as a ghostwriter.

When I wrote the first edition of this book in 2009, I focused on the opportunities for writers who wanted to write books for clients. In the past four years, however, there's been an explosion in the need for ghostwriters, especially those who write blogs, articles, and other pieces like case studies and white papers. That's what we're now calling content marketing.

Yet even savvy writers don't think about these opportunities, or they don't know how to find them, or they don't know how to sell themselves as ghostwriters, or they don't know how to work as a ghostwriter/content marketer.

This book will help you do all that. You'll learn how to find ghostwriting opportunities if you're a book author who wants to add ghosting to your writing repertoire. You'll also learn how to locate and write shorter projects, and to develop steady ghostwriting clients.

Still on the fence? Jump off now, with these five solid reasons to add ghostwriting to your repertoire:

• **Larger range of potential clients.** When I started freelancing full-time 16 years ago, I could make a living writing for print magazines. After a year or two, I was receiving feature assignments where I was paid, say, $1.50/word for a piece of 1,500 words. That's $2,250 for a story—not bad at all. And I knew hundreds of other writers doing something similar, making six-figure livings (or close) writing almost exclusively for consumer magazines.

Those days are gone. Today's successful freelancer performs different kinds of work for a wide variety of clients, and is always striving to continue to develop his skills and expertise. The ability to ghostwrite makes you more valuable to the many clients who need writers who can do it.

"While I have no hard data, anecdotally it seems to me that ghostwriters may be in even more demand than they were in the past," says award-winning business and financial writer Randy Myers. "I think a lot of corporations are trying to leverage all the outlets for writing that are now available to them via the Internet and social media, even as many traditional print publications continue to shrink."

• **Increased client retention.** Both publishers and corporate clients like to work with freelancers who can do more than one thing; it makes their lives easier. Expanding your "scope of work" to include ghostwriting makes you more valuable to current and potential clients.

• **Steadier work.** Signing a new client is the most time-consuming part of freelancing. Even established writers spend between 20 and 50 percent of their time marketing themselves. Ghostwriting can help assure a steadier stream of work. When a client hires you to produce content for his website, for example, you may be looking at regular assignments every week or two, if not more often. This cuts your marketing time and ups your average hourly rate.

• **More money.** Do you blog already? Well, you can get paid more for ghost blogging. First, clients who hire ghosts tend to be "bigger checkbook" clients. Second, losing your byline usually means extra money from a potential client. And when you do a good job, clients want you to keep working for them, which means you're making more per-hour because you have to spend less time marketing yourself. (This is the corollary to the above point.)

• **Ongoing demand for ghosts.** As Myers mentioned, the trend of more people looking for ghosts is likely to continue. "Because there has been more reporting about ghostwriting arrangements—often that go awry, unfortunately—there is a greater awareness of ghostwriters and rising demand for our services," says ghostwriter Marcia Layton Turner, the founder and executive director of the Association of Ghostwriters. "More people are now aware that we exist and understand the role ghostwriters can play in crafting well-written content. For people who don't like to write or who don't have time to do it, ghostwriters can be a lifesaver.

"I think, too, that any stigma previously attached with using a ghostwriter is now nonexistent," she adds. "There is no shame in hiring someone to communicate your message because it's understood that the ideas and concepts are yours. In fact, in some circles, having a ghostwriter is fairly prestigious."

Let me be clear. I'm not saying you have to ghostwrite exclusively. Like most writers, I like writing in my own voice, and I still write my own books (like this one) and blog and write articles. But the lion's share of my work today is ghostwriting—because there's a demand for it; because it pays well; and because I enjoy doing it. Those three factors are the building blocks for any type of successful freelancing, regardless of what type of work you do.

The Big Gigs: Ghostwriting Books

So far we've talked about ghosting shorter pieces. But when most people think of ghostwriting opportunities, they think of books.

There's no shortage of authors and would-be authors in the United States. According to an oft-cited survey of more than 1,000 Americans, 81 percent claim "to have a book" in them. (Sounds painful, doesn't it?) At least six million Americans have already written a book.

And plenty of books are being produced. According to Bowker, a company that tracks publishing trends, in 2011 alone, more than 345,000 print books were published (including more than 143,000 which were self-published), along with more than 87,000 e-books.

That's a lot of books, and it means that in any given year, there are several million people spending thousands of millions of hours writing their books. As a ghostwriter, you don't really care about those people—unless you happen to be one of them. The people you do care about are the people who want to write a book but lack the time, skills, dedication, or all three to do it. That's where you come in.

As a ghostwriter or coauthor, you don't write your own books. You write other people's books—because that's where the money is. But I've found that even seasoned freelancers often know little about ghosting books, unless this kind of work is already part of their business plan. If you're new to the field, you may not have even considered ghostwriting and coauthoring as a way to make money as a freelancer.

I certainly didn't. I started my freelance business after "escaping from the law" in 1997. I was a former attorney with a creative writing degree but no practical journalism experience. It took me about 18 months to build my business to the point where I wasn't riddled with fears of having to take a part-time job at Starbucks to support my new career, or worse yet, having to return to the law.

But in the meantime, I broke into dozens of national magazines, cranked out articles of all lengths, and saw my income steadily climb. I decided to specialize in health, fitness, nutrition, and relationship subjects and began developing solid relationships with editors and clients. I had started teaching writing classes, was speaking at writers' conferences, and was finally making enough money that I was certain I could continue to freelance, save for retirement, and have plenty left over for delivery pizza and decent pinot grigio.

But it wasn't enough. I still dreamed of writing something more substantial. I wanted to write a Book. I kept my desire to myself, however. Over the first four years of my fulltime career, I'd experienced multiple failed attempts at novels, all of which featured an unhappy female lawyer as the lead character (a coincidence, really!) and I didn't think I could write a book. Books were—well, they were just too long. Books involved hundreds of pages, tens of thousands of words, and major commitment.

I admit it—I have a short attention span. I get bored easily. And besides, I was a magazine writer. I banged out four-paragraph queries in fifteen minutes or less. I outlined articles in my head. I could approach any topic in 300 words, 800 words, 1,500 words—whatever my editor wanted. That was my lot as a writer.

Then one day I had an epiphany. You know what a book is? A bunch of chapters. And you know what a chapter is? A long article. Hence:

A book = a bunch of long articles.

Wait a minute. I could write a long article! And I could write a whole bunch of long articles! I'd already done that. So I could write a book after all.

Over the course of a weekend trip to New York, I started working on the idea for my first nonfiction book. I wrote a proposal which netted me my agent, but never sold. My second book, however, did sell. And then I managed to finish and sell a novel (featuring not one, but two unhappy female lawyers! Double the misery! Double the angst! Double the drama!), and realized I wanted to continue writing books.

My Introduction to Ghosting

It was at this point, about five years into fulltime freelancing, that I heard a speaker who would eventually change the course of my career. The late Sarah Wernick was a longtime member of the American Society of Journalists and Authors ("ASJA") and a well-known coauthor who had worked with a number of experts to write their books. Her first book, *Strong Women Stay Young* (with Miriam Nelson, M.D., a researcher at Tufts

University) was a *New York Times* bestseller and launched her successful coauthoring/collaborating career.

During a panel at ASJA's annual writers' conference, Wernick talked about how she identified and contacted experts who could be potential collaborators. Each expert had to have a significant, marketable platform (there's that word again!), and some kind of book-worthy idea. (Wernick was savvy about scouting experts, and identifying these book-worthy ideas—often before the expert herself did.) She then worked with the expert to create a book proposal, for which she was paid, and wrote the book with the expert once the pair received a book contract.

Two things stood out in my mind listening to her brief yet info-packed presentation:

1. **She was making a six-figure income doing this.**
2. **She was stuck having to write someone else's book.**

My reaction was immediate, and visceral. But I don't want to write someone else's book! I want to write my own books! Sure, it was working for her, and a six-figure income had been one of my goals for a while. But I didn't want to be tied to an expert for a year (or more) and have to write a book that I had little or no interest in. (I penned articles all the time I had little or no interest in, but hey, they were short assignments, not a long-term commitment.) Wernick's words and her cheerful intelligence did make an impression, but her no-nonsense approach to making money writing didn't appeal to me.

Fast-forward several years. I was still cranking out articles for print and online markets, and I was writing books as well. I wanted to ditch articles to focus on books, but I wasn't making enough on writing books to do so. Why not? Because my hourly rate on books was so low.

As a freelancer, I was used to being paid by the word (say, $1/word and up for national magazines and big websites, $0.50/word for trades and smaller sites, and maybe $0.10-0.25/word for regional magazines) for articles. But I also knew that it wasn't dollars/word that determined how much money I could make, but dollars/hour. I took (and still do take) assignments that paid far less than $1/word, for example, because I knew I would make a reasonable hourly rate on them.

For example, I have a market that paid a mere $.30/word. Many established writers might scoff at such an assignment because of the "low" rate. But this magazine covers one of my specialties. I email a list of one-line story ideas and my editor assigns the ones she wants me to cover, which slashes my marketing time. Because I'm an expert in the area, many articles require little background research, and the ones that do take a couple of telephone or email interviews which may total an hour before I actually write the piece.

I also know that a typical 1,500-word piece for this market will take me several hours, plus another hour to edit and proof. So, I'm making $450 for about four to five hours of work, which translates to $90 to $112.50/hour, right in the $100/hour range I aim to make. (Remember, I've been doing this for more than 16 years, and my hourly rate goal has increased significantly from the $20/hour or so I wanted to make when I started out.)

Also, because I know what my editor wants, rewrites are all but non-existent. This means no "after-time," which keeps my hourly rate down. Contrast this example with another magazine I've written for, except this one pays $1/word, a typical starting rate for national consumer publications. My last feature for it included a query, a revised query, a detailed outline, a revised detailed outline, about four hours' worth of background research and reporting, at least a dozen telephone interviews with both expert and "real people" sources, and two revisions including one which involved completely reorganizing the piece. We're talking about 40 hours' worth of work (over the span of five months) on a piece that started out as a simple, straightforward piece I expected to take about 10 to 15 hours. While I was paid $1,500 for the story, my hourly rate was less than $40/hour...to say nothing of what I call the PIA (that's polite for Pain In the...) factor. Assignments like that one may produce a fat paycheck but at what cost?

To pitch and write an article, as a freelancer, you:

1. Originate an idea. (Caffeine always helps me here.)

2. Research the idea and find some kind of hook for your pitch.

3. Locate a potential market for the idea (unless you already have one in mind).

4. Write a compelling query geared for your target market.

5. Determine who the appropriate editor is for your pitch (if you don't know who it is already), and make sure you have his/her current contact information.

6. Send your pitch.

7. If you receive no response, follow up on the query.

8. If you receive the assignment, discuss the article assignment with your editor. (If you don't, resubmit the pitch to another

potential market.)

9. Following the specs of your assignment, do additional research for article, including identifying experts and other potential sources.

10. Contact and interview sources, and conduct any other relevant research.

11. Write initial draft of article.

12. Edit, proof, and finish article and turn it in.

13. Wait for "great job—your check is on the way," or "nice work—go ahead and send an invoice." If you hear the dreaded words, "you've got a great start here, but…," or worse, "I'm not sure what's wrong with this piece but it's just not working for me," prepare to revise.

14. Conduct additional research and interviews, if necessary.

15. Rewrite article per editor's specifications.

16. Turn in article and return to step 13.

17. Receive payment (hopefully promptly).

18. Review galleys and/or answer additional questions from editor once the story goes through its final edit, if necessary.

19. Receive copy of magazine in mail or link to story online, and share with your sources.

It's a lot of steps for a check, isn't it? That's why I cut corners to save time—by doing things like specializing in a handful of subjects; "reslanting," or spinning off ideas wherever I can; developing regular clients who give me frequent assignments; and selling reprint rights to articles that have already been published.

But when we're talking books, the list of steps to publication and payment is even longer, at least in the world of traditional publishing. [We'll talk more about different book publishing options in chapter 8.] First, to sell a nonfiction book, you'll have to write a book proposal. (More than 90 percent of nonfiction books are sold on the basis of a proposal, not a completed manuscript. If you're selling a novel, however, you'll have to have a finished manuscript before you start pitching agents and/or publishers.)

So, if you want to enter the world of nonfiction book writing. Prepare to:

1. Come up with a compelling book idea.
2. Research the market to determine what the competition is.

What books are already in print that are similar to yours? How will yours be different, and better than, its competitors?

3. Write a book proposal, which includes the following elements:

- The **overview** of the concept and a brief statement of your qualifications;
- The **audience**, which describes the target market (in other words, who will buy your book);
- The **"about the author"** section where you highlight your "platform" (more about that in a bit);
- The **competition analysis**, where you list competing titles, and describe how your book differs from them;
- A **marketing and promotion** section that describes how you will use your platform, connections, social media, and marketing savvy to help sell the book;
- An **outline** of the book, which includes brief chapter summaries and other material the book will include (i.e., foreword, appendix, and index);
- At least one **sample chapter** (often two, if you're an unpublished author); and
- Relevant **attachments**, such as magazine articles you've written about the topic.

Sound like a lot of work? It is. My book proposals usually take four to six weeks to write, depending on the subject matter and amount of research I have to do, and run between 30 and 60 pages. One coauthored proposal, which included detailed chapter summaries, weighed in at more than 120 pages and was written over the span of nearly six months.

4. Research possible literary agents (if you don't have one, and want one) and/or possible publishers for your book.

5. Contact literary agents and/or editors at publishing houses with a query letter, asking if they're interested in seeing your full proposal.

6. If/when you receive interest from agents and/or editors, send the book proposal to them.

7. Wait (and sometimes wait, and wait) for responses from agents and/or editors.

8. If an agent offers to represent you, and you want her to represent you, sign an agency agreement. She then sends the proposal to

editors at publishing houses. (If no agent agrees to represent you, or you want to sell the book on your own, send the proposal to any editor who requests it.)

9. If (and that is a big if) an editor at a publishing house wants to buy the book, receive an offer for the book, either directly or through your agent.

10. If you accept the offer, you receive a publishing contract for your review and signature. Depending on the terms of the contract, accept your first advance payment—and try not to spend it all immediately.

11. Research and write the first draft of your book. (Give yourself at least six to nine months, depending on your deadline.)

12. In the meantime, start working on your marketing and promotion plan you described in your book proposal.

13. Revise, edit, and proofread the book. Turn in the completed manuscript.

14. Wait to hear from your editor.

15. Continue working on your marketing/promotion plan.

16. Receive revision requests and questions from your editor. Address them as necessary, and turn in the (new) final manuscript.

17. Depending on the terms of your publishing contract, receive (and spend) another advance check now that the manuscript has been accepted.

18. Review and make any necessary changes/corrections to the copyedited manuscript.

19. Review and make any necessary changes/corrections to the galleys, or page proofs.

20. Continue working on your promotion plan (hopefully in conjunction with your publisher's publicity department) like identifying and contacting possible book reviewers, bloggers, magazine editors, and social media mavens; setting up speaking appearances and book signings; pitching related articles; and basically attempting to get as much publicity for your upcoming book as possible.

21. Receive your actual book in the mail! Take time to Tweet, blog, update your status on Facebook, email, call friends, brag to your enemies, and celebrate your "baby."

22. Spend every waking moment (at least it will seem like that) for the next three months (minimum) promoting and marketing your book, with the assistance of your publisher's publicity department (hopefully).

23. During the coming months, continue to market your book by sending press releases, harnessing social media, writing articles about the subject, responding to interviews, making appearances, going on television and radio programs, podcasting, putting up videos on Youtube.com, speaking at various events, wearing T-shirts to trigger interest in the book (I've done it!), mailing postcards, you name it… all while still running your freelance business so you can make money. Because none of this time-consuming publicity—which you have to do to sell your book—actually pays money.

And I've reached my point, at last. **People assume the most time-consuming part of "writing a book" is writing the book. It's not. Selling the book will devour even more time.** And that's where writers go wrong. Let's take one of my own books as an example. I received $15,000 (an average advance for a midlist author like me) for a book about one of my specialties. Because it was a topic I'd written about before, the proposal didn't take as much time as I'd originally expected—about 25 hours, including the time to research the competition and develop my marketing plan.

When I received the contract, I started writing the rest of the book. In addition to doing some background research, I interviewed two dozen key sources, and wrote the remaining ten chapters in the next six months (while juggling other assignments, most of which were magazine articles). Including the research and interviews, writing the entire book (which includes the dedication, acknowledgements, and index) took about 110 hours. (This was a relatively "fast write" for me. Normally writing a book would take at least twice as long but I had a lot of material already at hand—columns and articles that I'd written and owned the rights to—that I could revise and adapt for the manuscript.)

Happily my editor was pleased with the initial draft, and I only had about seven hours' worth of changes to make per her suggestions. Reviewing the copyedited manuscript took about four hours, as did reviewing the galleys (and yes, I still missed two typos!).

Total time: 150 hours (so far)
Hourly rate: $100/hour

Not bad, right? But I'm not done with the book by a long shot. Starting about six months before publication date, I was pitching related articles, lining up speaking gigs, and looking for other ways to promote the book. When it came out, I devoted even more time to selling it to potential readers.

Let's just assume that for the six months before publication and for the three months thereafter, I devoted, on average, five hours/week to book marketing. That's five hours/week, for 39 weeks, for another 195 hours so far. Now we're looking at:

Total time: 345 hours (so far)
Hourly rate: $43.47/hour

And while my publisher may not be interested in doing much to promote the book after the first three months post-publication, I'm going to keep promoting it. After all, I want it to sell, and I want it to "earn out," so I can make royalties. But there's no guarantee that that will happen. After I receive my first six royalty statement, I find that I've sold around 4,600 copies of the book, producing royalties of just over $5,000. Good news, right? Well, yeah—but remember that my advance was $15,000. That means that any profit is offset by my initial advance, so I'm still in the hole for another $10,000 before I see any more money. So I continue to promote and market the book whenever I can, all while my average hourly rate for this book continues to plummet.

Despite my committed marketing, I may never see royalties. And if I don't—after all, most books do not earn out—I'm getting a set amount of money for all of this work, regardless of how many hours I spend promoting it afterwards.

That is why most is why authors don't make decent money writing books. There's an innate conundrum in this publishing setup:

1. To sell your book, you must commit substantial time to marketing it.

2. The time you spend marketing will not pay off in actual dollars (unless you eventually make royalties), forcing you to either work more to make up the difference, or to take a cut in your income—or both.

A Ghost Is Born

As a freelancer-cum-author, I'd noticed that my annual income had stagnated—yet I was working more hours than I had since I first launched my business. What was happening? Well, while I was working more hours than before, I was getting paid for fewer hours because of all the marketing/promoting time I was devoting to my books.

That was when I suddenly thought of Sarah Wernick, and how she approached her business and I had another epiphany. Sure, she was "stuck" writing someone else's book. But when it was finished, she was free! She didn't have to spend the next three to six months (or more) of her time promoting a book, which meant her income was suffering along with her mental health.

Finally, the penny dropped. I still wanted to write books, but now I saw that the benefits of collaborating or even ghostwriting might indeed outweigh the drawbacks. I decided to stick a toe into the coauthoring pond and see what happened.

Alas, my first collaboration attempt wound up circling the drain (more about that later) but my second was lucrative, interesting, and worthwhile. I thoroughly enjoyed working with my coauthor, and decided to make collaborating and ghosting a regular part of my writing repertoire. I've never regretted it.

Best of all, ghostwriting can be lucrative, even while the average advances given by traditional publishers are dropping. Here are some fees I've received for ghosting projects:

- $20,000 for a 60,000-word book for a nonprofit organization.
- $15,000 for a 40,000-word book for a book packager (the author already had 14,000 words but needed to expand it to a full manuscript).
- $15,000 for a 60,000-word book for a private client. The client wrote draft chapters and I rewrote and reorganized the material for clarity, cohesiveness, and tone.
- $12,000 for a 55,000-word book; I worked as a developmental editor on a manuscript that needed tuning up, editing, and rewriting for voice and flow.
- $25,000 for an 80,000-word book for an expert who had a contract with a major publisher; my client wrote about one-third of the manuscript while I wrote the rest and edited her section for style and consistency.
- $4,500 for a book proposal (this is a little low for a proposal fee, but I was familiar with the material and really wanted to work with this client).
- $10,000 for a 70,000-word book. This project was a mistake, in retrospect; I expected it to have great "back end" potential and agreed to a low fee for half of the royalties. Well, so far there have been no royalties. This is a lesson I learned

the hard way.

- $22,000 for a book proposal. That's not a misprint. Writing the initial proposal involved wading through 700 pages of scientific material; the proposal was eventually expanded to become more than 100 pages. Originally written for $15,000, I asked for and received $7,000 more for the additional work.

An informal survey of other writers reveals similar fees. One frequent ghostwriter is making $15,000 to $25,000 for books of 50,000 to 75,000 words. Another just made $12,000 for a 30,000-word book. A third made $22,500 for a 65,000-word book and $13,000 for a 60,000-word book where the author had provided a "very rough" draft of the material. A long-term ghostwriter of books has seen her average rates fall from $20,000 to $25,000 pre-recession to $8,000 to $18,000, but remains busy with work.

"Today a larger percentage of my income comes from ghostwriting," says Turner. "Today I'd say 80 percent+ of my income is from ghostwriting books and blog posts. Recent projects have averaged $30,000-$50,000. My rates have gone up a little, mainly because I've been so busy that I'm less focused on trying to be the low bidder. I quote fair fees and now lose some because I'm not bidding $10,000 for a project that should cost several times that."

While rates may not be as high as they have been in the past, there is plenty of money to be made, and an ever-growing list of potential clients as well. A salary survey several years ago found that ghostwriters with eight years' experience average $60,000 a year. More recent stats indicate an average yearly income of about $80,000, but many ghosts make well over six figures annually.

There are other benefits to ghosting books, too. If you're working with a subject matter expert or well-known person, it's likely you'll get a bigger advance (even if you only receive part of it) than for a book under your own name. Today publishing is driven all by platform. Forget your idea, no matter how compelling it is. To get a book contract, you'll need platform, and the bigger, the better. Your platform is essentially what will help you sell books—it's your name, your reputation, your audience, your blog, your followers on Twitter, your media connections, you name it.

As a freelancer, chances are your platform isn't too big. Unless you're a celebrity, a well-known expert in a specific field, or you happen to be the recipient of raunchy texts from Elliot Weiner, your platform isn't going to be much to Tweet home about it. On the other hand, your expertise in a certain subject area can help you obtain work that requires a background in the subject. Still another benefit to ghosting is that you can write about anything you want without diluting your own platform. You could be a well-known fundamentalist Christian author and ghostwrite a steamy bodice-ripper on the side—without anyone being the wiser!

Another huge plus is that once the book is done, it's done. As you just learned, with your own manuscript, writing the book is only the beginning. Any author will tell you that the real work begins when your book comes out and you have to promote and sell it to readers! As a ghost (and usually as a coauthor, too), when the book is published, it's up to the author, or "name," to sell the book. Whether it sells ten or ten thousand copies isn't up to you—and if it doesn't sell well, those poor sales figures won't hurt your chances of selling your books to publishers in the future.

For all these reasons—and maybe additional ones specific to you—it's smart to consider "disappearing" and becoming a ghost.

Chapter 2

Can You Disappear?
Determining Your Ghosting Potential

After reading chapter 1, you may be thrilled about jumping into the ghost-writing field. Let's make sure you're qualified to do so first.

Here's the thing. Yes, ghostwriting and writing are similar. But not everyone who writes can ghostwrite—or wants to. Good ghosts do more than write without bylines; they're able to channel their client's voice, in a sense, and craft prose that always keeps their client's goals in mind.

If you're able to do that, you should be able to ghostwrite shorter pieces. If you decide to ghostwrite books, however, you need to be able to do more than write in a specific voice.

The bottom line is that this field isn't for every freelancer. Strong writing skills are a given, but there are other attributes that are essential to succeed in this particular specialty. The first has to do with ego. You may be committing months to this project, but it's not your book—it's your client's. Even when you collaborate and your name appears on a book cover (almost always below the author's name and in significantly smaller letters), the book will reflect your client, not you. And it should. When you ghost or collaborate, you are expected to "disappear" and let your client's voice shine (while you do all the behind-the-scenes work).

That's why ghosts typically don't have big egos. Or, if they do have big egos (yes, I admit that I have one too), they're able to set them aside during the writing process. Repeat after me: this is not your book! It is your client's. And you have to be able to help create, develop, and deliver that manuscript.

Willing to set your ego aside? Great. Then how are your organizational skills? It's one thing when you're researching and writing an article or even your own book, but when you work with someone else, you have to have some kind of system. You must stay on top of your own research, organize information you receive from your client, track various drafts (in progress or approved), and manage a schedule that may be ever-changing depending on your client's needs. If you work for more than one client at a time (which is likely when you freelance), you also need strong time management skills. Chances are, however, that if you're already a successful freelancer, you have plenty of practice juggling multiple assignments.

Another attribute that cannot be overlooked is patience. If you work for a "PIA" editor occasionally, your contact with the person is limited. But when you ghost or collaborate, you may be stuck with that person for months. Some clients will decide on a plan of action, and then follow it to the letter. (I like them a lot!) Others will second-guess their decisions, want to change the scope of the book as you're nearing completion, or need continual handholding.

Your patience (and sanity) may be tested when you have a client with a bad case of what I call the OMTs, or "One-More-Thing." You think you're done with a chapter (and the client has signed off on it), and guess what? Two weeks later, your client decides the chapter needs reworking.... or wants to add another anecdote....or wants to reorganize the entire book. This is a bigger issue when you're working for a set fee as opposed to an hourly rate, where you can just charge the client for the additional work. That doesn't mean it's any less of an annoyance.

Another consideration? Your personality type. Let's say you're a "type-A" time-oriented, driven person like me. What happens when you agree to ghostwrite for a client who's much more laidback about deadlines, whether it's failing to provide you with necessary information or "forgetting" to put your check in the mail? What if you abhor conflict and you sign with a client who loves to argue over every minor point?

This is especially something to consider for book projects. You and your client don't have to score the same on the Myer-Briggs personality test (in fact, it's probably better if you don't), but your personality, attitude, and flexibility will impact how you work with clients. The most successful collaborating relationships (both ghosting and coauthoring) I've had have been ones where I "clicked" with the client immediately. In other situations, I knew almost as quickly that there was no way I wanted to work with this person for an hour, let alone a year. And then there have been others when I heard that little warning voice but signed anyway. Let's call those "life lessons" instead of big fat mistakes.

Ghostwriting also requires a high level of creativity. If you're writing a memoir, a novel, or "creative nonfiction," you'll need a narrative arc and an overall theme or message for the book. Even a relatively straightforward how-to article requires an ability to organize material, structure the piece, and identify and maintain your client's voice.

Ghosting isn't simply a case of filling in an outline, or connecting the dots. You need problem-solving skills, too. A talented ghost brings more to the table than writing ability; he or she brings fresh ideas, brainstorming skills, and a collaborative spirit to make the piece that the client wants to write even better—without being asked.

For example, when working on a book on the psychology of successful sales coaching, my client had already written a section on the importance of listening to the members of your sales team. Yet he hadn't addressed exactly *how* to be a good listener. I did some background research on active listening, and added a section to the chapter in my client's voice that explained what active listening is and how to use it, along with specific examples. My client liked the addition and it made that chapter more useful for readers. For a how-to book, that is essential.

Another example? While working on a book proposal for a dietitian, I suggested that we incorporate "real people" anecdotes to exemplify some of the nutritional problems she wanted to address. Real-life examples make potentially dry information more compelling, and give readers people they can relate to.

Finally, if you want to ghostwrite books in addition to shorter pieces, you need working knowledge of the publishing industry. You need at least one published book under your belt to attract clients. Have you written multiple book proposals? Do you have an agent? Have you worked with different editors at more than one publisher? Do you know the difference between traditional publishing, self-publishing, and print-on-demand ("POD") and the advantages and drawbacks of each? The more experience you have with books, the more valuable you are to a client. (Remember, I didn't even consider getting into collaborating until I had published both fiction and nonfiction books on my own—and learned a lot about publishing in the process. Since then, I've worked with publishers, self-publishers, agents, book packagers, and private clients, and each experience deepens my knowledge base in some way.)

Can You Wave "Bye-bye" to Your Byline?

We've covered some of the traits of a successful ghost. Wondering how you rate? To get a handle on your potential for successful ghosting, take the following quiz. It's designed to test attributes like temperament, flexibility, time management skills, and publishing knowledge. The first nine questions address your general ghostwriting potential; the last six will help determine whether you'd be good at ghosting books:

1. After putting in 25 hours on a 1,000-word story for a new-to-you editor, she emails and asks you to completely rework the piece. You:

A. Agree, and turn it in three days later—you expect some rewrites with a new client.

B. Agree to do the revisions, and withhold judgment until you do another piece for her.

C. Tell her she should have been more specific in her assignment letter, grudgingly do the revisions, and vow never to write for her again.

2. Having to write in a publication's voice that differs from your own is:

A. No problem.

B. Sometimes a challenge, but you're always willing to try.

C. Time-consuming—you have a distinct voice that is difficult to tweak.

3. You've rescheduled an interview with a key source three times now—and when you call, she's unavailable yet again. You:

A. Immediately tell your editor what's happening, and line up a backup source in case the source "flakes" yet again.

B. Try her one last time, and then ask your editor how he'd like you to proceed.

C. Become annoyed, delete her contact info, and contact a fill-in source you think will work.

4. Asked to come up with a "fresh" approach to an evergreen story subject, you:

A. Immediately start brainstorming—it's one of your favorite things.

B. Review your portfolio for possible ideas.

C. Sigh heavily. Isn't that your editor's job?

5. You're offered a project but the rate is below what you're usually paid. You:

A. Give the potential client three solid reasons to boost your pay.

B. Attempt to negotiate more money, but take the assignment even if you can't get more.

C. Turn down the assignment—you have your standards.

6. How many different markets have you written for?

    A. Ten or more

    B. Five to nine.

    C. Less than five.

7. How much do you know about content marketing?

    A. I've done some already, and want to do more of it for clients.

    B. I'm interested in breaking into this writing niche.

    C. Pretty much nothing.

8. How proficient are you working with Word?

    A. Very—I can track changes, insert tables, graphics, and photos, and create footnotes and endnotes.

    B. Somewhat—I have a decent understanding of the software.

    C. I'm the writer...aren't tables, special formatting, and the like my editor's job?

9. Your closest friends say...

    A. You never forget a thing...you have dirt on them from your college years.

    B. You're a good listener if you're not distracted.

    C. You tend to tune out if you're not interested in the conversation.

10. When asked, you could give five excellent reasons to work with a traditional publisher...and five excellent reasons to use POD instead.

    A. Of course—you have experience with both publishing avenues.

    B. You're biased toward one, but know the difference between the two.

    C. You're familiar with one kind of publishing, but not the other.

11. How many books have you published?

    A. Four or more.

    B. Three or fewer.

    C. None.

12. As a freelancer, you:

    A. Balance your work and personal lives fairly well.

    B. Sometimes find it challenging to meet deadlines and still have time for family, friends, and other obligations.

    C. Constantly struggle with work/life balance and work nearly every weekend.

13. You get into an argument with a close friend, and it gets personal. He apologizes and you:

    A. Forgive him—reasonable minds can differ.

    B. Forgive him but rehash the fight with your better half.

    C. Shrug it off, but never call him again. Life is too short to deal with people who don't see life the way you do.

14. The idea of writing a book on a topic you know nothing about:

    A. Excites you—you like to explore subjects in depth.

    B. Is overwhelming—I'd have to break the book into smaller chunks to get a handle on it.

    C. Terrifies you—you're afraid you'd lose interest by the third chapter.

15. AP versus Chicago…which one uses the serial comma?

    A. Chicago.

    B. AP.

    C. AP versus Chicago what?

Give yourself one point for every A answer, two points for every B answer, and three points for every C answer. If your score totaled 15-20 points, ghosting and coauthoring is probably a natural fit for you; between 21 and 33 points, it's a possible option; and if your score is more than 34 points, you're going to have to work harder than most to succeed in the field.

The Ghost Inside You

As a ghost, you must be able to "channel" your client, capture and retain his or her voice, and create a piece (whether a brief article or a 75,000-word book) that meets his expectations. Your ability to do this, and do it well, depends on a multitude of factors. Personality characteristics like temperament and drive are all but impossible to change. (I try to be more easygoing, really. But I can't morph into a "type B" no matter how much yoga or deep breathing I do.)

However, marketing yourself, managing your time, writing in someone else's voice, and organizing material logically are *skills*—skills that can be learned, and improved upon. You can also educate yourself about publishing, learn how to negotiate a ghost-friendly collaboration agreement, promote yourself, attract clients, mange your workload, and build a successful career as a ghostwriter and collaborator.

Keep reading—this book will help you do all of that.

Chapter 3

Go Where the Money Is: Pursuing Ghostwriting Clients

Okay. You've got an idea of what ghostwriting entails, and you think you've got the skills to start doing it. What comes next? Finding clients.

We'll talk about clients for shorter pieces—e.g., articles, blog posts, and other content marketing work—first, and then move into books later in the chapter.

Corporations/Businesses

Let's start with the biggest opportunity for ghostwriters today—the thousands of companies, websites, and online publications that hire writers to produce copy ranging from web pages to articles to slide shows to electronic magazines ("e-zines") and more. Much of this work now falls under a new name—"content marketing."

"Most professional writers are already doing some form of content marketing writing and don't even realize it," says Jennifer Goforth Gregory, a freelance content marketing writer. "A good example of content marketing is American Express OpenForum. Ultimately, American Express wants to increase their business credit card customers. But instead of simply directly marketing their cards to small businesses, they created a very informative website for small business owners. The result is that small business owners now regularly visit the site and owners now associate American Express with understanding the needs of small business owners.

"Content marketing writing is any deliverable that is part of a brands content marketing strategy," continues Gregory. "A freelance writer might be hired to write a white paper or create a loyal following on a blog geared towards the brands target customer. But beyond these somewhat traditional deliverables, freelance writers are increasingly involved in other forms of content marketing deliverables, including infographics, video and even text for content marketing-related apps."

Pros: Number one, there's plenty of this kind of work for savvy writers. In 2012 alone, corporations spent more than 40.2 billion dollars on content marketing, and that figure is likely to climb. While pay rates vary, many online markets pay $0.25 to $1/word for content.

Cons: The markets that pay well are often inundated with freelancers who want to write for them, and turnaround times can be tight. Depending on the client, you may have more than one "boss" to please as well, so expect rewrites, at least when working with a new client.

Marketing your mastery: Look for potential clients that will appreciate your background and experience. Pitch the potential client with a strong letter of introduction ("LOI") demonstrating your expertise and highlighting your knowledge of the company or site.

"LinkedIn is a goldmine for finding out information about prospective clients. One way is to browse open job positions using the key words "content" and "content strategist," says Gregory. "You should also search for "copywriter" since many content marketing gigs are mistakenly listed as copywriting positions. Another way to use the search feature is to search for companies within your niche that have positions with the word content, such as Content Marketing or Content Strategist. If a company has a position devoted to content marketing, then there is also a good chance that they may have a need for freelancers now or in the future."

Blogs

More freelancers are adding ghost-blogging to their portfolios, possibly because it's one of the easier ways to break into ghostwriting. You do need to have blogging experience, but my annual income survey of freelancers reveals that nearly half are blogging for pay. A background in blogging and expertise in a particular area can get your foot in the door. That's how Erik Sherman started ghost-blogging for a corporate client.

"That came about because they needed someone to ghost-blog in the area of IT [information technology], an area I regularly cover," says Sherman, an author and ghostwriter. "It started as an experiment...but it's turned into six posts a month on different topics." While he had done some ghosting before, it was his knowledge of IT that interested the client—and led to a long-term assignment.

If you're not lucky enough to have work come to you, think about how you can "sell" your experience to potential ghosting clients. For example, if you're written about health for consumer magazines, you can ghost-blog for health-related sites. If you write about business, look for blogs that cover the trades and industries you know about.

"If you have your own blog, it's great to do guest blogs," says free-lance copywriter Kelly Kautz, who ghostwrites for marketing companies. "And once you're ready to take that step into ghostwriting, find people in your area who would really appreciate a service like that. Blogging is a great way to get clips and demonstrate your ability [to ghost-blog]."

Pros: There are thousands of blogs that pay for posts, and the fact that they must be continually "fed" (i.e. updated) means they are constantly in need of writers. Most blog owners don't want to work with new writers all of the time—they'd rather have a "stable of writers they can rely on, and once you've proven yourself, you have an ongoing assignment.

Cons: I've found that blog posts don't pay quite as well as other on-line content—anywhere from $25-30 to $300+ for a post of 500-800 words. Your clients may also ask you to provide images or use SEO (search engine optimization) terms in your posts, which means they may take a little more time to produce.

Marketing your mastery: You may already be following some blogs you want to write for. To find more markets, use Google to search for blogs in the subject area you write about. Check the blog's guidelines to see if its owner accepts posts, and whether (and what) it pays.

"I have found ghosting gigs though my network," says freelanc-er Jill Russell Qualizza. "Entrepreneurs are looking to build network on LinkedIn, Facebook, and Twitter, and use a blog as their main content portal. Companies or individuals that want to promote their businesses through blogs and traditional media coverage need writers. Some are even in need of writers for guest posts on other people's blogs. And it isn't just original writing; I am finding work by editing other guest posts for the same blogs."

Instead of sending a query, consider writing a blog post and submit-ting it to the editor as many blog editors prefer this. If you do query with a specific topic to cover, highlight your knowledge of the blog's subject area, and your own blogging experience to get an assignment. Otherwise use an LOI customized for the blog you're pitching.

Custom Content Producers

You may have already heard of custom magazines, or written for them. A custom magazine is a hybrid of sorts. It looks like a consumer magazine but it's aimed at a specific audience, often the customers of a particular company. For example, Walgreens offers customers magazines including *Happy and Healthy* and *Diabetes and You;* GNC has *Muscle & Body;* and the Vitamin Shoppe has *Muscle & Performance.* Custom publishers create magazines, websites, and other pieces for corporations, non-profits, and other clients who use these publications to help strengthen their brand and develop customer loyalty.

Writers may not consider this kind of work ghostwriting, but in many cases articles are not bylined—or they contain bylines of company execs or experts. I've written for more than a half-dozen custom magazines, usually getting my foot in the door with an LOI that highlights my experience instead of a query.

Pros: Custom content companies usually pay per-word, and their rates are comparable to consumer magazines. Expect to be paid $0.50-$1/word and up.

Cons: Freelancers in the know pursue this kind of work because of the relatively high rates, so competition can be stiff. And some smaller custom content publishers don't pay quite so well—I've seen a few companies with rates as low as $0.10-0.25/word.

Marketing your mastery: Ask friends and family to collect custom magazines for you, and check market guides like *The Standard Periodical Directory*, which lists thousands of potential markets. And check out American Business Media, which maintains a searchable database of custom content producers. Use a query or LOI to make your initial intro.

PR Agencies

Public relations, or "PR" agencies, hire freelancers for ghostwriting projects, including content marketing. "Content marketing is basically PR ghostwriting. In other words, you are writing an article that ultimately benefits a business, industry or individual company or service. It is PR disguised as journalism...without a byline," says Qualizza. "You are still researching a topic, still finding top-tier experts and still writing a well-balanced article, but the main difference is that you are promoting a product or service and working to motivate your audience to a preferred call to action—whether that is buying said product or service."

Randy Myers has had bylined pieces in *Wall Street Journal, Barron's, The New York Times*, and numerous other business and financial publications. He also ghostwrites for PR agencies and corporate and institutional clients. "In a typical scenario, a PR agency somewhere learns about my work from seeing my byline in a magazine, and hires me to ghostwrite an article for one of their clients," says Myers. "Sometimes, it's someone in the company's PR department who makes the initial contact." Myers then interviews the client by telephone, and writes the piece. He charges per-word for articles.

"This usually allows me and the client to agree on a firm price in advance," says Myers. "For example, an exec wants an article ghostwritten for a trade magazine; the magazine says it wants 1,000 words, I multiply my per-word rate by 1,000 and give the client a firm price."

Pros: Once you get in with an agency, you may get work without having to do any more marketing—busy agencies need writers that can turn around work quickly. You're typically paid an hourly rate (think $25 and up) but you may be able to negotiate a per-word rate for projects instead.

Cons: Agencies typically pay lower rates than you would receive working for a client directly, and turn-around times can be tight. Some agencies may expect you to come in to meet with potential clients or to participate in meetings while others simply want you to provide what they asked you for on time.

Marketing your mastery: Create a list of ad agencies and send an LOI that details your writing experience. And ask other writers and graphic designers who freelance for ad agencies if they're willing to share contact names, and be willing to return the favor.

"I've found content marketing work with corporations and PR agencies," says Qualizza, who has ghostwritten as both a staff writer and a freelancer. "Working for a corporation, we use content marketing in lieu of traditional advertising…Companies are looking for and are hiring writers that are reporters by trade, but can flip into PR marketers in the end."

Book Ghostwriting Clients

The bar is higher to ghostwrite books than shorter pieces. Ideally you're already a published author. The more you know about publishing (for example, how traditional publishers acquire titles and the pros and cons of using a print-on-demand publishing company), the more valuable you are to clients, and the more likely you are to find work.

If you want to ghostwrite books, you have plenty of different types of clients to choose from. Book publishers, literary agents, book packagers, corporations, associations, celebrities, subject matter experts, and people from all walks of life hire ghostwriters. The type of people you work with and the type of ghosting work you do may depend on your experience, background and personal interests, but an understanding of the clients ghostwriters work for—and how to connect with them—is essential to your success.

Everyday Joes (and Janes)

Let's start with the most "basic" ghostwriting client. This is the person who simply wants to write a book. He's not a celebrity, or an expert, and he doesn't have a contract with a publisher or an agent pushing him to write a book proposal. For some reason (possibly many reasons), he wants to be an author. But something is standing in his way. Maybe he doesn't have the time. Maybe he doesn't have the patience. Maybe he doesn't know enough about writing—or maybe he simply can't organize his material into an actual book. Or maybe he's written a book (or something roughly resembling one) but needs help with structure, organization, tone, you name it.

He has figured out, or at least suspects, that he can't do it alone. So he's decided to find a ghostwriter to tell his story, or help him tell it. He (or she) is who I call the Everyday Joe, or EJ.

There are more EJs out there than any other kind of client. Here's the thing—nearly *everyone* thinks he has a book in him. (Remember that 81 percent of people say *they* should write a book. In fact, there are more people who believe they should write a book than there are people who actually *read* books—according to a recent survey, just over half of Americans read a book in the last year. Scary, huh?)

But let's get back to our EJ. He's got a book to write. He may even think it's a bestseller in the making. That's fine. What isn't fine is when he expects you to be paid *when* the book becomes a bestseller. Be afraid when you hear phrases like "*Everyone* says I should write a book," "no one would believe the story of my life," or "I've got the makings of a bestseller right here" (as he taps his temple and gives you a knowing look). I've heard all of this (every ghostwriter has) and more.

But as a ghostwriter, you shouldn't care about your EJ's story, or even its bestselling potential. You *should* care about his budget—namely, does he have one, and how big is it. Because if this person has no money, chances are you aren't going to work with him. (Okay, I'm going to make an exception to this rule—if he is Oprah's secret love child, has the DNA test to prove it, and wants you to tell the untold-story of his life. Then I'll tell you to get an ironclad ghostwriting agreement, write a book proposal for nothing, and hang on for the ride.)

But ordinarily, EJs have to have money (and be willing to spend it on you) to be viable clients. Many don't. But some do, and some will pay (even pay well) to get their words on the page. The vast majority of the inquiries I get from EJs do not turn into work. But some do, and the sheer number of potential clients makes pursuing them worthwhile.

Pros: As I just mentioned, there are tens of millions of EJs who want to write books. With the explosion of POD and other author-driven publishing options, the number of book authors is skyrocketing—and some of them actually realize that if they're not professional writers, they need some kind of assistance with their books. The subject matter of these books is as varied as the clients themselves; you may work on memoirs, novels, cookbooks, histories, business books, or how-tos.

While many EJs don't have money, others do—and this work can be lucrative. Journalist, author, and ghostwriter Jill Amadio specializes in private autobiographies, memoirs, and biographies for EJs, many of whom are retired and want to tell their life stories. Her fees range from $15,000 to $45,000 per book. She aims to write two books a year along with other freelance work, which provides her with a comfortable living.

Cons: For every 100 people who want to have someone write their book, just a fraction—let's say three percent—have the money and *are willing* to pay to have someone actually do it. EJs may need more handholding than other clients, and may not appreciate the amount of time and experience it takes to bring a book to life. They can get excited about a project only to lose interest after a few weeks or months, or insist on working for a percentage of future profits or some other nebulous figure.

Marketing your mastery: Amadio finds work through job boards like those run by the American Society of Journalists and Authors (www.asja.org) and the Author's Guild. (http://authorsguild.org). She has also advertised in markets where wealthy seniors, who make up the bulk of her clientele, live.

But personal referrals are Amadio's biggest sources of work. "Tell your friends, neighbors, and colleagues," says Amadio. "Word of mouth brought me a client who'd just bought a mansion from my Realtor buddy; another lead came from my doctor's receptionist."

To reach EJs, take a broad approach to marketing your ghostwriting business. Your website or blog, your email signature, your bio note on the articles you write, word of mouth, and social media can all help you find clients. [More on these techniques in chapter 4.] Looking for and responding to advertisements on craigslist.org and other sites may also turn into work. Teaching classes and leading workshops on book publishing (even at your local library) can raise your local profile and help you find clients.

Pros with Platforms

This type of client is arguably the best source of work for ghostwriters. The Pro with a Platform ("PP") is often a businessperson who doesn't just want to write a book; she wants to add "book author" to her CV, or curriculum vitae. Maybe she's establishing herself in a particular profession and knows a book will build her credibility. Maybe she's a motivational speaker who wants to boost "back-of-the-room" sales. (In addition to speaking fees, speakers make money by selling books, DVDs, and other products to attendees.) Maybe she's a plastic surgeon or an investment advisor or a personal trainer who knows a book will help her attract more clients. Whatever the motivation, the PP wants to write a book but lacks the ability and/or time to do so.

PPs are my favorite kind of clients. They tend to be smart (at least about their particular subject area), and often respect the time, brainpower, creativity, and experience it takes to ghostwrite or collaborate on a book.

PPs often look for ghostwriters who already have some knowledge of their subject area. If you've specialized either as a magazine freelancer or book author, this can set you apart from other ghosts. Ellen Neuborne, a New York City-based ghostwriter, specialized in business topics as a newspaper and magazine staffer and freelancer. "I find having a specialty is extremely helpful in ghostwriting," says Neuborne. "Clients want to make sure that you 'get' their topic. They don't just want a good writer. They want a soul mate for their book. A specialty is like a credential. It says: 'I care about your topic and am as attached to it as you are.'"

Professional writer Graciela Showalter started her ghostwriting career creating consumer-oriented articles for a health website. "My name never appeared on these articles or anywhere on the website. Each article was carefully reviewed by a team of physicians, who made corrections as needed. Their names appeared at the end of the article instead of mine. So I was ghostwriting without knowing it!," says Showalter. "Nowadays, I'm comfortable ghosting articles and blog posts for many clients, including motivational speakers and technical experts. They have the expertise; I simply put it in writing for them."

Pros: On average, PPs tend to have bigger budgets than EJs, likely because they look at a book as an investment in their business, and are more willing to pay for a ghostwriter or collaborator as a result. If you have experience in a certain subject area (business, health, or technology, for example), you're more valuable as a ghost to clients who need someone who understands their field. And once you've done a book for a PP, your name tends to get passed around to others in the profession. (My two best sources of referrals are both PPs who are well-connected businesspeople. They're constantly giving out my name to colleagues who say they want to write a book. That's great news for my business.)

Cons: Just as with EJs, some PPs mistakenly believe that you'll make money on the back end—you know, when the book becomes a bestseller. You'll set them straight, of course. Another real drawback is that the busier a PP is, the less time she may have to dedicate to her book project—or she may require you to be available at odd times. Successful PPs may have sizeable egos that make them challenging to work with, but I've found than any potential drawbacks are far outweighed by the benefits of working with PPs.

Marketing your mastery: To reach PPs, play up your background and experience, especially if you specialize. When you write magazine articles and get a bio note (the brief line at the end of an article about its writer), identify yourself as a ghostwriter. And let sources for your own books and articles know that you ghostwrite and collaborate on books.

If you want to meet potential PPs, you need to network, whether online, in person, or both. "Referrals are my best source of work," says Neuborne. "So I work hard to meet agents and packagers. I attend conferences...I participate in the ASJA Personal Pitch [which lets ASJA members meet editors and agents face-to-face] every year and I use it just to hand out my resume and say: 'I'm a ghostwriter. If you have a project in need of my services, please call me.' I've gotten good work that way."

Book Publishers

Traditional book publishers often hire ghostwriters to pen books for "name" authors, whether celebrity bios (or autobiographies), business tomes, or novels. Publishers with book series or popular authors hire writers to supply a steady stream of books for their readers. (Robert Ludlum, who died in 2001, is still churning out books. And best-selling author Robert Patterson works with ghosts and collaborators who follow his outline, then return the drafts for his review and approval.) Editors hire ghostwriters or collaborators to work on books that the authors can't handle on their own; in some cases, they don't discover this until late in the game and a writer is hired to finish a book that's way behind schedule.

Sharon Cindrich, a parenting and technology expert and writer, had written a book for Random House when she decided to pitch her next project to American Girl, the company which publishes "Smart Girl Guides" aimed at preteen girls. She's since written two books for American Girl, and has found working for a "branded" series has multiple advantages.

"Considering the length of the books and the work involved, the advances have been excellent," says Cindrich, author of *The Smart Girl's Guide to the Internet* and *The Smart Girl's Guide to Style*. "Another huge advantage is that the company has such a strong brand, the books almost sell themselves—and that means I'm more likely to make royalties on each title. With these books, I'm not expected to spend all my time marketing the books when they come out—American Girl does that, and does it extremely well. At this point in my career, I don't care if my name isn't actually on the cover [it does appear in the book], but I care about making a living, working on meaningful projects, and continuing to build my platform as a parenting and technology expert. And writing for AG has been a way for me to do that."

As an author, simply marketing your own books, either on your own, or through an agent, can lead to coauthoring or ghosting work. Magazine and newspaper journalist Tim Gower writes about health and medicine, and his first collaboration came about unexpectedly. "I've been doing a lot on dietary supplements—herbs, vitamins, the whole bit—and I put together a proposal for a user's guide of the 100 most widely used supplements," says Gower, coauthor of books including *The Sugar Fix* with Timothy Johnson, M.D. "My agent shopped it around and found a publisher who said they liked the proposal, but would like it even more if I had an MD after my name."

Fortunately the editor had just received a proposal from a physician, and suggested Gower team up with him. While Gower calls it a "shotgun marriage," the first collaboration led to other ghosting and collaborative work, including a half-dozen books for *Reader's Digest*.

Pros: Once you have your foot in the door, book publishers can keep you busy with ghosting and collaborating work. Depending on the project, publisher, and deadline, you may be looking at fees in the mid-five-figures and up. Working for a publisher, you may be able to negotiate royalties (as opposed to a flat fee) for book projects. And if you ghost or coauthor a book that becomes a bestseller (or at least does well enough that the publisher wants a follow-up), you're likely to be the first writer who gets a stab at it—assuming the author is willing to work with you again.

Cons: It's hard to crack this market unless you've already written for traditional publishers, have publishing connections, or both. These projects often require fairly tight (sometimes extremely tight) deadlines. And while there are still good deals to be had, some projects don't pay that well upfront. (If that's the case, try to get a share of the royalties.) Another potential drawback is that when you're hired by a book publisher, you have no say in choosing your client—you have to "make it work," as fashion expert Tim Gunn would say, with whoever the expert or celebrity is.

Marketing your mastery: You have to be a book author to sell publishers on your ghosting skills—and editors often want you to have prior ghosting or coauthoring experience as well. If you specialize, play up your unique background to set you apart from other ghosts. Look for editors and publishers who produce books in your area of experience, and send an LOI, or letter of introduction, that describes your experience.

The best resource to promote your ghosting/coauthoring business to editors is Publishers Marketplace, www.publishersmarketplace.com, or "PM," the site for learning more about book deals, agents, editors, and the state of the traditional publishing industry. For $20/month, you'll receive the daily *Publisher's Lunch*, an email newsletter, and be able to post your own listing promoting your ghostwriting business. Plus, you can research publishers, editors, and agents, and search for information about the last ten years' worth of reported publishing deals. This is invaluable not only for learning about publishers that may hire you but also when you're working with PPs and EJs who may want to market their books to traditional publishers.

Book Packagers

Book packagers are similar to book publishers with one primary difference. Traditional book publishers offer a contract (that usually includes an advance, even a small one) for the right to publish a book. A packager is paid by someone else to publish a book—often an individual or in some cases, a publisher that has hired the packager to create the book that the publisher will then sell.

Packagers like to work with ghostwriters they know can deliver a manuscript on time, so once you've proven yourself, you're likely to get more work. "The writers who work for me over and over again are very flexible and understand the business of ghostwriting. Some of our clients get busy with work. They go on business trips and the book takes a back seat. These aren't things we can control or schedule, but it happens a lot," says Leah Nicholson, project manager at Jenkins Group, Inc., a book packager. "My favorite writers can roll with these delays. They have other projects (books or articles) to keep them busy."

Pros: When writing for a packager, you don't have to worry about setting a budget or getting money from the client—while you're working with the author, your client is actually the packager. "The writer doesn't have to worry about collecting the money or taking the risk," says Nicholson. "*We are also responsible for sorting it out if the project is canceled. We do our absolute best to make sure everyone walks away whole.*" Fees range across the board, but some of these projects can be lucrative depending on the client, the type of book you're doing, and how long it takes you to complete it. I've seen packagers offer in the mid-five-figures for business books, and in the $15,000 to $40,000 range for books on other subjects. It's the client's budget (either the individual or publisher that has hired the packager) that sets the fees.

Cons: As Nicholson mentioned, you can't always control the availability of the author you're working with. That means you may be stuck with someone who's hard to reach, hard to deal with, or both. And some packagers offer ridiculously low fees. (I've had offers as low as $2,500 for all rights to an 80,000-word manuscript.)

Marketing your mastery: Book packagers are often looking for potential ghostwriters. Research packagers and send an LOI highlighting your subject areas of specialty, asking that you be kept in mind for possible jobs.

"I look for someone who is tailor-made for the client. By the time I'm searching [for a ghostwriter] for a client, I have a good understanding of what the client is looking for in a writer," says Nicholson. "Obviously, it is important to me to find a writer who has experience writing on the topic of the book. It makes the learning curve much shorter and the project can get off the ground faster."

If you respond to an advertisement for a particular job, make sure that your LOI is customized for that project. "Typically, I've posted an advertisement for the position. That ad lists what the job's responsibilities and writer requirements are," adds Nicholson. "I really love introduction letters that tell me exactly how the writer's skill set matches with the requirements for the job. Be confident. Tell me how exactly you're going to knock it out of the park!"

In addition to using Google to find book packagers, check out the Association of American Book Producers Association's website, www.abpaonline.org, for a list of members.

Literary Agents

There are big changes afoot in the publishing industry today. Ten years ago, you could sell a book on the basis of a good idea and some knowledge of the subject. That's no longer the case. Today it's all about platform, and literary agents know this. But their clients who have strong platforms may lack essential writing skills (or the time to sit down and write a book), so they often work with ghostwriters to write the book proposals which will hopefully result in lucrative book deals. Then the author often uses the same ghostwriter to pen the book itself.

Just as with publishers, you've got to have some ghostwriting experience—and a good reputation—for agents to consider you for projects. Literary agent Claire Gerus finds potential ghostwriters by word of mouth, and references from other agents and authors. "I might even ask an editor who they've worked with who is in that genre that I'm looking for, whether it's health or business or whatever—military, political—so I like to get references," says Gerus, president of Claire Gerus Literary Agency. "I would hesitate to just go on some sort of website and pick anybody from a particular category."

Even so, to make sure the ghostwriter is a good fit for her client, Gerus sometimes asks ghosts who are new to her to prove their mettle. "That might mean sending, say, a sample chapter to a ghost or to a free-lance writer and saying, 'how would you rework this?'" she says. "I don't expect them to do the whole chapter for nothing, but certainly a few pages in I'll be able to know whether they've got the right feel for it and so will the author…so, definitely doing little test runs is a good idea, I think."

That test run helps Gerus determine whether she has the right ghost for the job. "I find that experience is key, and also the ability to morph into someone else—to almost be a chameleon as a writer and be able to get into the head space of the person you're working with, and yet refine what that person would have done," says Gerus. "It's a pretty magical quality and not everybody has it."

Pros: Agents understand that to sell a book to a traditional publisher, their client must have a well-written proposal. Average fees for proposals for nonfiction books have slipped a bit in the last couple of years, but in most cases you're talking in the $5,000 to $10,000 range. An agent isn't going to invest time in a client she thinks can't sell a book, so your chances of a book proposal turning into a book contract are higher than if you write a proposal for an individual who's sought you out. And if an agent likes your work, she'll use you again—and may pass your name on to editors or other agents looking for ghostwriters.

Cons: Typically the expert/author is the one who pays for the book proposal. If the expert understands that the proposal is an investment in his career and is willing to pay for it, great. But I've been asked by agents to write full proposals for as little as $1,500. Another drawback is that a client may not be willing to agree to have you write the manuscript if the book sells—or the editor may have her own ghostwriter or collaborator she wants to bring in. (So, if you want to ensure that you'll be writing the book itself, make sure your contract with the agent and author says so.)

Marketing your mastery: This is a harder area to break into because most agents already have ghostwriters and collaborators that they've worked with before. But if you have a background or experience in a particular area, it's worth pitching agents with an LOI if they represent authors who write books about related subjects. And of course if you have an agent for your own books, let her know that you're interested in collaborative work.

Finding agents who use ghostwriters and collaborators takes legwork. Agents won't always state on their websites whether they work with ghostwriters or coauthors, but reviewing the books they've represented can help you determine this. (Check the acknowledgments where authors thank their editor, their agent, their coauthor or ghost, their spouse, their mother, and the like. Also look to see if a coauthor's name pops up more than once—that's a good indicator that the agent has clients who use coauthors and ghostwriters.)

Literary agent Linda Konner says that at least 75 percent of her clients' books are ghostwritten or coauthored. "I have developed a solid base of cowriters/ghostwriters since I started my agency in 1996. I couldn't function without them," says Konner, president of the Linda Konner Literary Agency. When she started her agency, she used word of mouth to find potential ghostwriters and collaborators. Today when she has a client with a strong platform who lacks the time or ability to write a book, she matches that person with one of her stable of collaborators.

In addition to simply checking the bookshelves, there are both print and online guides to help you locate potential agents. Some of the best include:

- *Guide to Literary Agents 2014*, Chuck Sambuchino (Writers Digest Books, 2013);
- *Jeff Herman's Guide to Book Publishers, Editors, and Literary Agents 2013*, Jeff Herman (Sourcebooks, 2013); and
- *Writer's Market 2014*, Robert Lee Brewer (Writer's Digest, 2013)

Two worthwhile online resources include:

- www.publishersmarketplace.com Yup, I'm plugging PM again. For $20/month, you can search member agents, get more information about their clients and recent deals, and stay up on what's happening in the book publishing industry.

- www.agentquery.com/default.aspx While geared toward writers seeking agents for their own book projects, this site includes hundreds of agents along with advice about submitting work, resources for writers, and general publishing info.

And of course, don't forget to Google the agent's name. In addition to her website, you may come across interviews and other relevant information to help you pitch her.

Corporations/Organizations

Both nonprofit organizations and corporations use ghostwriters for book projects, including company histories. These books usually represent a significant investment for the company or nonprofit, and can be quite lucrative for writers hired to do them. Kathi Ann Brown, president of Historical Milestone Consultants, writes corporate and organizational histories and family histories, and her fees range from $25,000 to $150,000, depending on the scope of the work involved.

Brown's first project fell into her lap; she was finishing her master's degree in history when a friend from college asked if she'd be interested in writing the 75th anniversary history of a big engineering company where his brother-in-law was marketing director. "Before I knew it, I was hired and off and running," says Brown. "It took me about 15 months from start to finish, including traveling around the country to interview 30+ members of the firm. I loved it!" She works as a writer, not a ghost (she's credited on all of her corporate/organization histories) and says that the ability to research is essential to succeed in this niche.

"To do the job right, you need to be prepared to dig, dig, dig, and learn, learn, learn. And then do it some more. If you don't enjoy research, you probably won't enjoy writing history," says Brown.

Writer and author Heidi Tyline King, who has been freelancing since 1993, started doing corporate histories about ten years ago. Her first grew out of a project she was doing for a local hospital. "I'd been doing brochures and other work for them and they wanted to do a 40-year history and asked me to do the book," says King. "That gave me a corporate history I could show to other clients."

While it's easy to think that corporate histories are one-size-fits-all, that's a misconception, says King. "Some companies just want the facts— 'we did this, we did that'—but I like to turn into a story, and I like to have different voices [in the history]," says King. "I will interview everyone from the CEO to the janitor…but I understand that with this type of writing I'm at the mercy of the client—my job is to make them happy."

For example, one recent project involved a history for a professional organization. "It was a ghostwriting project, and the outgoing president wanted to leave his magnum opus before he retired, and to make sure that history was told from his perspective," says King. "So my job was to take what he said and make it readable content. But the next client I worked for really did want to make the history more objective. So you have to ask whether they want to tell 'their' story or the 'real' story. It's very different than a history or biography you're writing for yourself—you are beholden to the client."

In addition to experience writing corporate histories, Marian Calabro, the president of CorporateHistory.net, often hires freelancers for these jobs, and has a specific skill set she looks for. "Essential: excellent research, interview, and client relation skills, plus the ability to write engagingly about people and business, and to write precisely to an assigned word count," says Calabro. She also prefers that writers have book-length writing experience, corporate writing background, and some knowledge of the particular client's industry.

Pros: This is a specialized field, but corporate histories and other ghostwritten projects can spell big bucks for ghostwriters. Once you've done one and have a sample of your work, you can use that to market your experience to other potential clients.

Cons: Like working with book publishers, this market is tough to break into if you lack experience. While many of these projects offer big paychecks (think $50,000 and up), the work often entails months of re-search and interviews. "The overriding priority is a 100 percent comfort level with the realities of corporate communications," says Calabro. "*The client has the final say.* If you can't live with that or will privately complain about it throughout the project—and these projects typically last for one to two years—then don't take on a corporate history, at least with us."

Marketing your mastery: A business-writing background certainly helps when it comes to writing corporate histories or doing other ghosting projects for companies and nonprofits. Use your experience in a particu-lar trade or industry as a calling card. King writes articles for association magazines on corporate histories to help get her name in front of potential clients, and maintains contacts with companies that write corporate histo-ries like Calabro's, which hire writers on a freelance basis for projects. Once you have at least one corporate history under your belt, an LOI to those companies may pay off with work. These companies include:

- Corporate History.net (www.corporatehistory.net) (Calabro's company)
- History Associates, Inc. (www.historyassociates.com)
- Moment LLC (www.momentllc.com)

Finally, keep in mind that decision-makers at corporations tend to move slowly. "Corporate histories involve what salespeople call 'long-cycle selling," says Calabro. "It can take months if not years for clients to move from inquiry to contract. I'm currently talking with a company that first called us in 2007, then in 2009. They're still figuring out whether and how to move ahead."

Chapter 4

Market Your Mastery:
Selling Your Ghostwriting Skills

Last chapter you learned about the types of clients you may work for, and how to reach out to them. But that's only the beginning of selling yourself as a ghostwriter. In this chapter, we'll first talk about how to market yourself as a ghost; then we'll talk about how to find shorter ghostwriting gigs (i.e., articles, blog posts, and corporate pieces). Finally, we'll talk about marketing yourself as a ghostwriter of books.

Spread the Word:
Marketing your Ghosting and Collaborating Business

Some clients lend themselves to particular kinds of marketing. Regardless of the type of work you do, however, there are a variety of ways to promote yourself and your ghosting/collaborating skills. Most successful ghosts use a mix of techniques to help them stay busy with work. In general, the more you do, the better—consider how Ellen Neuborne markets her ghostwriting business.

"I do cold mailings to agents and book packagers," says Neuborne. "I also make sure everyone I know knows what I do. I have 'ghostwriter' in my email signature. I have it on my business cards. I think too many freelance writers would like to be ghostwriters, but they don't make that intention clear on their marketing materials. I make it clear on everything I use to communicate that ghostwriting is my primary job. I also maintain a blog about ghostwriting [www.ghostwritingrevealed.blogspot.com], and I teach an online class for writers looking to break into ghostwriting."

The below techniques will help promote your ghosting business to clients:

Your website. At this point, I can't imagine any successful self-employed writer not having a website. It's that essential. But your website doesn't have to have a lot of bells and whistles to attract clients. It should include: a description of the kind of services you offer; a list of prior projects; client testimonials, if you have them; and a brief biography.

Melanie Votaw's first ghostwriting gig came about through her website. "I'd written books of my own and wanted to expand my writing work, so I put on my website that I did ghostwriting," says Votaw, a ghostwriter, author, and editor. "That was seven years ago." Her first project was a dentistry book, and since then, much of her work has come through her site and word of mouth.

Your blog. I resisted jumping on the blogging wagon, hoping it would fade away before I had to embrace it. However, much like the victims of the Borg on *Star Trek*, resistance was futile. I have been assimilated. If you're going to blog, however, consider whether and how your blog will market your writing business. Some people (gasp) blog for fun! That's not me. My blog, http://dollarsanddeadlines.blogspot.com, has a specific audience—nonfiction writers who want to make more money in less time. But it's also designed to promote my work as a ghostwriter and collaborator and attract more clients.

Professional writer Graciela Sholander takes a similar approach with her blog, http://ghostwritingplus.wordpress.com/ask-me/. "I always advise writers to create an online presence. My blog is one significant component of my online presence; others include my website and a Facebook page," says Sholander. "Through my blog I post short articles and blurbs covering topics that matter to ghostwriters and their clients. When people come across my blog by doing Google searches on ghostwriting-related topics, chances are they'll click on my name, which I link to my website."

Jennifer Goforth Gregory's blog about content marketing, www.jennifergregorywriter.com/blog, is an excellent resource for freelancers, but it also raises her profile and attracts clients. Even if you don't have your own blog, posting on ghostwriting and writing-related blogs can get your name out and help establish yourself as a ghostwriter.

Your email signature. Every time you send an email, you have the opportunity to market yourself. Create an email signature that includes your title or description of the work you do. Here is one of mine:

> Kelly James-Enger
> Ghostwiter/Author/Speaker
> Owner, BodyWise Consulting
> www.becomebodywise.com

Gregory makes sure that the phrase "Content Marketing Writer and Copywriter" appears in her email signature. "This is an especially effective technique if you are working with sources for trade publications, consumer magazines or websites who may also have content marketing needs," says Gregory. "For example, I write articles for several publications and websites geared towards hospitality professionals, which is an area I have significant industry knowledge. Earlier this year, I got a writing assignment from a B2B hospitality company who I worked with on an article simply because I had included Content Marketing Writer in my email signature. And be sure to include a link to your website so that potential clients can see your work."

PublishersMarketplace.com. If you're going to be in the ghosting biz, a subscription to PM is essential. In addition to using it for research, you should maintain a listing promoting your ghostwriting business. Take Neuborne's PM listing, which is succinct, and professional: www.publishersmarketplace.com/members/Eneuborne/.

Bio notes for articles. Your magazine and newspaper work can also help you attract clients. "My target clients are business execs and entrepreneurs, and to a lesser extent, people who deal in investing topics," says freelance writer and ghostwriter Gwen Moran, coauthor of *The Complete Idiot's Guide to Business Plans*. "I write a lot for publications which target those audiences, so that makes me visible to these people." And business writer and ghostwriter Jacqueline Lynn's first ghostwritten book was the result of a phone call from an entrepreneur and attorney she'd met months earlier. When he saw her byline on a story in an inflight magazine, he called her about working for him. This is why you cast your marketing net wide— you never know how you'll catch a potential client.

Writer's organizations. Organizations like the American Society of Journalists and Authors ("ASJA") (www.asja.org), the Authors Guild (http://authorsguild.org), and the Association of Ghostwriters (www.associationofghostwriters.org) post jobs for member ghostwriters and coauthors.

"The AOG continues to attract more experienced ghostwriters, which may be why we're seeing an uptick in the quality of projects brought to our members. We've had agents for celebrities hunt for ghostwriters in our midst, which is great," says Marcia Layton Turner, its founder and executive director. "I think one of the biggest benefits for members—aside from the monthly teleseminars, newsletters, and discussion forums—is the member directory, which has allowed clients to approach members directly about their projects. I know several members who have landed significant projects simply by having their bio listed in the online directory. That's new since last year. But we also get at least a project a week, on average, from would-be authors who use the AOG Find a Ghostwriter service to try and track down the right ghostwriter."

Satisfied clients. Clients who are happy with your work are one of the best ways to market yourself. When you complete a project, ask that they keep you in mind if they know of other people looking for ghostwriters, and if they're willing to serve as a reference in the future.

Randy Myers ghostwrites articles for corporate clients, usually for publication in trade magazines or business newspapers, or the websites of those publications. "Sometimes, PR agencies bring that work to me, other times, corporations already familiar with my work hire me directly. Some of that work also comes from referrals from editors and writers I've worked with in the past," says Myers, who also writes white papers for corporate clients.

"As is the case with most of my assignments, this work usually comes from clients who already know me and call me when they need something written—or from referrals," he adds. "Typically, clients already familiar with me have seen my byline somewhere, perhaps in an article in a *Wall Street Journal* special advertising section or in a newsletter for one of the trade associations to which they belong. After nearly three decades in this business, they may have worked with me while they were working for a previous employer."

Article and book sources. Award-winning author and ghostwriter Stephanie Golden's first book collaboration came about as a result of profiling a woman for a magazine. Later, when the woman decided to write a book, she called Golden. The pair coauthored two books together and Golden's written books for other experts since then. I interview a lot of doctors, researchers, and health experts for my freelance work, and have gotten in the habit of letting sources know what I do in case they're considering writing a book—or know someone who is.

Teaching. Teaching classes whether in person or online can raise your profile and help spread the word about your writing business. Calabro teaches classes on business writing and email etiquette to staff at Columbia University and leads creative writing workshops at the Adult School of Montclair, New Jersey. I teach online ghostwriting classes and do webinars to let people know I'm a ghostwriter and coauthor in addition to writing my own articles and books.

Online job posts. Melanie Votaw has found work on Elance.com, a site that lets writers bid on a variety of writing gigs. "I occasionally bid on jobs on elance.com if they're halfway decent," says Votaw. "It's a bit like going into a thrift store—you have to really look through a lot of ripped and stained things before you find something decent." [Next chapter, you'll learn how to distinguish a promising potential gig from one that's a waste of time.]

One-on-one meetings. Every year, ASJA holds its annual writers' conference in New York. Members can attend "Personal Pitch" to meet editors and agents. I try to go every year for those invaluable one-on-ones.

If you do business writing, consider joining your local chamber of commerce, and attend meetings where you can meet business owners. Who you're looking to meet depends on who you write for. Take collaborative writer Ed Robertson, who has penned books about television stars and popular shows. Robertson currently lives in Los Angeles and attends television-related conventions to meet potential clients.

Networking. That means making connections, doing favors when you can, and simply creating relationships with people. "The most effective technique for me has been networking. I have a website and blog, but those generally serve more as a credibility builder once someone has been referred to me. I do my own business tips newsletter and put articles up on free article sites to keep my name out there," says Lynn. "Occasionally I will get an inquiry from someone who has found me on the internet, but so far that hasn't translated into any actual work. You have to get out there, tell people what you do (they are generally fascinated by the concept of ghostwriting and love to hear about it), and let them know you want referrals."

Social media has made networking easier than ever before, particularly business-related sites like LinkedIn. "I've gotten several content marketing writing inquiries from my LinkedIn page," says Gregory. "Make sure that you include 'Content Marketing Writer' in your professional headline as well as including your experience in the profile...My professional headline on my LinkedIn profile is Freelance Writer, Content Marketing and Copywriter.

"In the professional summary section, you should also include several sentences about your experience in content marketing writing. Write a summary that illustrates your understanding of content marketing and any specific content marketing skills you bring to a project, such as the ability to easily understand the needs of audience or your social media expertise," continues Gregory. "If you have a content marketing niche mention it as well as any relevant industry experience. Be sure to also include any content marketing skills or projects in the experience section for each of your past positions."

In addition to her blog about ghostwriting, Sholander maintains a ghostwriting Facebook page. "It serves dual purposes, namely, to serve as a valuable resource for ghostwriters but also to increase my online presence. I can't emphasize this enough," says Sholander. "The more online avenues you have to promote yourself as a ghostwriter, the better your chance of catching the eye of potential clients."

Advertising. When Kathi Ann Brown started writing corporate and family histories, she wrote articles, spoke at conferences and placed ads to promote her business. Jill Amadio advertises in publications that are likely to attract potential clients—well-off retirees. And Melanie Votaw has advertised her ghostwriting services on craiglist.org. If you advertise, think about the clients you want to attract, and what they're likely to read before you fork out the cash.

Local media. Amadio called her local paper and pitched herself as a possible feature subject. It paid off when the weekly paper ran a front-page piece about her. People are fascinated by writers and want to know more about their lives—I've been profiled by local papers three times. Come up with a compelling pitch for your ghosting business and send a press release to area publications—it may turn into excellent (and free!) publicity.

LOIs. Unless all of your work comes through referrals (lucky you!), you'll be sending out LOIs to potential clients. Just as a query letter sells an idea to a magazine editor, an LOI sells you as a ghost to client. You should have a template on hand that you can customize for potential clients, whether you're sending it to a packager, editor, or agent, or responding to an advertisement for a ghostwriter.

"I was fortunate to meet Robert B. Parker [author of the Spencer novels]—I spent an afternoon with him. He told me, 'you work with what you got.' I've always remembered that," says Ed Robertson. "I don't fudge my background but when I see an ad that I think I could fill the need for, I draw from what I have in my arsenal and present myself in the best possible way that would qualify me for the project." I take the same approach, starting with my "standard" letter and tweaking it for the project.

In my opinion, your LOI is your most critical marketing tool. With that in mind, I've included sample LOIs that you can use to help you create your own.

The first is from freelancer Jodi Helmer, who does a variety of work including content marketing. "I write a lot about farming and sustainable agriculture. I approached the editor of a custom publisher who oversees a magazine for an agribusiness firm. To let him know that I understand farming, I focused on the agriculture-related publications I've written for in the past," says Helmer. "In addition to highlighting my work in custom content creation, I also mentioned farming-related consumer publications."

Dear Mark,

I hope all is well. I wanted to send a quick note of introduction and express interest in writing for XYZ Magazine.

As a freelance journalist and author, I specialize in writing about sustainable living, including farming. I have written about topics ranging from carbon capture farming and livestock population trends to the downsides of urban agriculture and soldiers transitioning to farm careers.

In addition to writing for popular consumer magazines and websites such as Urban Farm, Hobby Farms, E: The Environmental Magazine, UrbanFarmOnline.com, HobbyFarms.com and National Geographic Traveler, I also contribute to custom publications, including Out Here (the magazine for Tractor Supply Company), GreenWise, Costco Connection and WebMD. In conjunction with UNC Press, I traveled to farms across Georgia and interviewed farmers as part of a forthcoming agritourism guidebook, Farm Fresh Georgia.

I understand the relationship between marketing and journalism and have a strong track record for meeting the needs of the client while producing content that is engaging for readers.

I welcome the opportunity to talk about your freelance needs. I'm happy to send writing samples upon request. Published clips are also available at www.jodihelmer.com.

I look forward to hearing from you and hope we'll have the chance to work together soon!

Best,
Jodi
[contact info]

Helmer uses the next LOI for custom publishers that work with healthcare clients, including hospitals. It highlights her experience and lets the editor know that she understand the difference between writing for a newsstand publication and producing content for a specific client:

> Dear Claire,
>
> I hope all is well. I wanted to send a note of introduction and express interest in writing for XYZ magazine.
>
> As a freelance journalist with a decade of experience writing about health topics, I offer the experience and passion it takes to turn the latest medical studies, health statistics and trends into articles that are both informative and interesting to read. I'm skilled at developing fresh story ideas, interviewing top experts, crafting copy in a voice appropriate for the magazine and I never miss a deadline.
>
> I understand the relationship between marketing and journalism and have a strong track record for meeting the needs of the client while producing content that is engaging for readers.
>
> My work has appeared in popular newsstand titles such as *Shape, Women's Health, Family Circle, Natural Health, Woman's Day* and *Arthritis Today*. I've also contributed health articles to numerous custom publications, including *Costco Connection, Caring4Arthritis* and *Restore*. Published clips are available at www.jodihelmer.com.
>
> I'd love to learn more about your freelance needs and hope we'll have the chance to work together to bring health and fitness articles to readers of XYZ.
>
> All the best,
> Jodi

This next letter is one that Jennifer Goforth Gregory uses for professionals like lawyers, doctors, and dentists. "That is an endless supply of content marketing work that is often overlooked," she says. "These professionals also often need ghostwriting for trade publications as well...to me, the most important part of an LOI for content marketing is the third sentence I have here, because it shows that you understand their client and what they are trying to accomplish with their content marketing. This is not something needed in a traditional LOI, but I think it's essential to a content marketing LOI."

Dear [Law Firm Contact],

I enjoyed working with you on the article for [Insert magazine name here] last year and wanted to touch base to see if you had any content marketing writing needs.

I have worked with several law firms and written content both for lawyers and clients. I am confident that I can create content that will help potential clients understand the law/legal system while increasing their trust in your firm's knowledge and expertise. I spent some time looking at your website and have several ideas for blog topics and case studies that will help your client's understand the legal system.

I have extensive experience writing content marketing deliverables for a variety of clients, including IBM, American Express, Adecco, Intuit and other law firms. I also have a solid understanding of content marketing strategy and blog regularly on the topic. My work has been published in *Entreprenuer.com, FOXBusiness, MSN Money, QSR magazine, Express OPENForum, Intuit Small Business Blog, Dice.com*, and over 50 different regional magazines. Additionally, I have a Masters degree in technical writing with a specialization in technology.

For the past 4 years, I have been a freelance journalist for the *Raleigh News & Observer*, a major regional newspaper, and have published over 200 stories—including many front of the section stories.

I am full of story ideas and often give colleagues ideas because I have more topics to write about than hours in the day. And you don't last three years as a correspondent for a daily newspaper without knowing how to meet a deadline. You can see what my editors have said about me on my LinkedIn Profile at www.linkedin.com/pub/jennifer-gregory/1a/551/9b8.

I look forward to hearing from you and hopefully working with you in the future.

Jennifer

I like Gregory's LOI at lot; it's both professional and warm. Next is a "cold call" letter I've sent to a book packager describing my background and experience:

Dear Mr. Lief:

I recently visited your website, and am writing to introduce myself in case you're currently looking for freelance authors/writers for your book packaging division. I write, ghost, and collaborate on book projects for packagers, experts, and traditional publishers.

A little about me: I've been a fulltime freelancer for the last decade. I started out writing for magazines, and since then, more than 700 of my articles have appeared in 50 national magazines including *Redbook, Self, Health, Family Circle, Woman's Day, Continental, Fitness,* and *Shape.* I segued into book writing about five years ago and am the coauthor of *Small Changes, Big Results: A 12-Week Action Plan to a Better Life* (with Ellie Krieger, R.D./Random House, 2005), a nutrition/fitness/wellness book; I'm also the author of five other books in print including *Six-Figure Freelancing: The Writer's Guide to Making More Money.*

In addition to writing my own books and collaborating with several co-authors, I've also ghosted several books. One was a book-length health care guide for the Joint Commission on Accreditation of Healthcare Associations; another was a book on sales coaching for a nationally-known sales expert. I've worked with hundreds of health, fitness, nutrition, and business experts over the years on projects including articles, marketing pieces, book proposals, and books. While I always consider the "voice" of my expert, I aim for a conversational, easy-to-understand style, which has made me popular with editors and clients.

I'm the owner of BodyWise Consulting, and speak and consult about subjects ranging from staying motivated to getting fit (I'm a certified personal trainer) to freelancing. I enjoy helping people make positive changes in their lives through my work as an author, journalist, and speaker.

Finally, I'm dependable, efficient, and never miss deadlines—all important attributes for successful collaborating and ghosting. I've dropped a brief resume below, and will be happy to send you writing samples if you like.

I'd appreciate it if you'd keep me in mind for future books that may be a good fit for my background and experience. I'd love to tell you more about my credentials if you're interested.

Thank you so much for your time, and have a great week!

All best,
Kelly James-Enger

This next LOI was for a particular project (RFPs, or Requests for Proposals), which I lacked experience with...so I played up the breadth of my background and reliability. If I did have the specific experience she was looking for, I would have opened with that, but instead I mention my corporate work and the "variety of projects" I've done. You've got to "dance with who brung you," so to speak—in other words, use what you have for an LOI:

Dear Nancy:

Patricia Bannan mentioned that one of your clients is looking for a freelance writer, and I'd like to introduce myself.

I'm a freelancer, ghostwriter, and collaborator and have worked on a variety of projects for publishers, corporations, experts, and private individuals.

A little about me: I left the practice of law to freelance fulltime in 1997. I started out freelancing for magazines, and more than 700 of my articles have appeared in 50 national magazines including *Redbook, Self, Health, Family Circle, Woman's Day, Continental, Fitness,* and *Shape.* A few years into my career, I started writing books, and am the author of titles including *Small Changes, Big Results: A 12-Week Action Plan to a Better Life* (with Ellie Krieger, R.D./Random House, 2005), a nutrition/fitness/wellness book.

In addition to writing my own books and working as a coauthor, I've also ghostwritten books, book proposals and other projects for clients. I've worked with hundreds of health, nutrition, fitness, and business experts over the years on projects including articles, marketing pieces, book proposals, and books. I have a conversational, easy-to-understand voice, which has made me popular with editors and clients.

Besides writing, I'm also the owner of BodyWise Consulting, and speak and consult about subjects ranging from staying motivated to getting fit (I'm a certified personal trainer) to freelancing. I'm dependable, efficient, easy to work with, and I've never missed a deadline. I've dropped a brief resume below, or you can visit www.becomebodywise.com for more about me.

Nancy, I'd appreciate it if you'd keep me in mind for this project—if you have any questions about my background or experience, I'd be happy to tell you more.

Thank you so much for your time, and have a great week!

All best,
Kelly James-Enger

Next is Ellen Neuborne's standard LOI, which is direct, professional, and brief; I like how she bullet-points her qualifications:

> Dear [ ]:
>
> Need a ghostwriter?
>
> I'm an experienced collaborating writer and I specialize in helping business people translate their ideas into book form. I have just closed my 10th book and I am on the hunt for new projects. If you have a client in need of a partner/writer, please consider me.
>
> Why hire me?
>
> • I am fast, accurate and organized. I can get a subject matter expert on a schedule and keep the project on track. My clients are busy people. I provide the structure and support they need to get a book done.
>
> • I am a versatile voice. I have written for publications as varied as *BusinessWeek, USA Today, American Baby* and Salon.com. I tailor my writing to the personality of my publication or co-author.
>
> • I provide a variety of services depending upon the client's needs. Some clients need a developmental editor to help map out the project. Others have a clear vision and need writing help. Still more are able to put the project on paper and need support getting the information into book format. I am experienced at diagnosing a client's needs and providing the necessary services.
>
> • Ghostwriting is my business. I enjoy the collaborative process and I am committed to it. There are many bright, creative people out there with books in their heads but without the time or skills to bring them to fruition. I consider myself a key link in the information economy.
>
> I am happy to provide writing samples and references.

Thank you for your consideration,
Ellen Neuborne
Writer*Editor*Ghostwriter

Ed Robertson's standard LOI showcases both his broad background and specialized experience. I especially like the way he includes links to relevant work and samples:

Dear _____:

I am a versatile, reliable award-winning freelance journalist with a proven track record in ghostwriting and book collaborations and a passion for the culture of the 1970s and '80s. I provide dynamic, marketable content for book and magazine publishers, literary agents, leading companies and executives from many fields. Memoirs, biographies, personal histories and narrative nonfiction are among my specialties.

I have had seven books published as an author, co-author or ghostwriter, including two books on the career of James Garner. In addition, I've written or edited hundreds of articles for print and online newspapers, magazines, custom publications, websites, video distribution companies and other media venues. My previous publishers include HarperCollins and John Wiley & Sons, while my previous collaborators include such *New York Times* best-selling authors as Jack Canfield, as well as such companies as Columbia House, The Wave Media, *The New York Times*, ABC Radio, CBS Radio, Warner Bros. Home Video, The Biography Channel and the TalkAmerica Radio Network.

I know how to create a compelling nonfiction narrative. My books on Garner, for example, provide readers with a portrait of who Jim is as a person, how he approaches his craft, and why he commands the respect of filmmakers and filmgoers alike. Time and again Garner has shown himself to be a man of principle who is not afraid to fight for those principles. In my books I make this come alive by telling stories that depict key events in Jim's life in which he has stood up for his own rights or the rights of others. I do this in such a way that Garner and the other people portrayed all emerge as fully-rounded "characters." These events not only humanize Garner, but connect the reader emotionally to Jim by showing him to possess many of the same heroic qualities of the characters he plays on film.

As a result of my books on film and television, I've been tapped as a consultant, researcher and onscreen commentator for several documentaries, including "Hollywood Maverick," an hour-long look at the career of James Garner that airs regularly on the Biography Channel and Turner Movie Classics, as well as "Who Shot J.R.?: The *Dallas* Phenomenon" (a featurette produced by Warner Bros. Home Video that discusses the popularity of Dallas in the context of the Studio 54 era), "Time's Up," a show on ageism produced by E! Entertainment Television, and "Married With Children: A Look Back," a forthcoming special that will also air later this year on The Biography Channel.

I am also a successful book doctor/consultant. Authors and agents recruit me to polish, retool or (in some cases) rewrite book proposals and manuscripts and make them marketable for mainstream publication. My credits in this capacity include *Big Brown: The Untold Story of UPS*, a combination biography of UPS founder Jim Casey and history of UPS and its corporate culture. In the case of this project, the author's agent felt the original manuscript was too dry and insular to appeal to a broad readership. I was hired to reconceptualize as well as rewrite the manuscript prior to submission to publishers. After working with me, the agent was able to sell the manuscript to a major publisher, and the book continues to perform well.

In addition, I host and produce a radio talk show about television that features interviews with celebrity actors and other entertainment industry professionals. Given the format of the program, as well as our key demographic, we often showcase classic shows and stars that appeal to the Baby Boomer era. Many of the interviews I conduct provide not only an overview of the guest's life and career, but a capsule history of the culture of the 1960s, '70s and '80s. In that respect, the show is biographical in nature as well as historical.

I am a member of the American Society of Journalists and Authors, the leading organization of independent nonfiction writers in the United States, as well as the Authors Guild, the Editorial Freelancers Association, and the Bay Area Editors Forum. A copy of my resume appears below. Additional information on my background can be found by visiting my website, www.edrobertson.com.

As an established biographical writer, I excel at developing material from my clients into compelling, marketable books for publication. I like to delve into subjects and especially love the era of Studio 54. I would welcome the opportunity to help you tell your story, should my background be of interest.

Regards,
Ed Robertson

Finally, here's one of Melanie Votaw's LOIs. I like Melanie Votaw's lead (Who wouldn't want to skyrocket their career?) and how this letter sets out her specialties, expertise, and experience. Highlighting the fact that she's written bestselling books will definitely help her stand out from other writers, too:

Dear _____:

I am a full-time freelance writer/editor/photographer and publishing industry consultant with 11 non-fiction books under my belt—some written under my own name and some as a ghostwriter. I would love to speak with you about working together on a book project that would promote your brand and skyrocket your career.

Why am I singularly qualified to help you with your book? *52 Weeks of Passionate Sex*, one of my early books, sold out its first printing to the stores within a week of its release, and my book, *The Cocktail Kit*, sold more than 100,000 copies. I have ghostwritten books on a variety of subjects, including medicine, dentistry, and popular business. One of these books was published by Hyperion, the publisher owned by Disney. Additionally, I have particular expertise in subjects related to dance, alternative health, psychology, spirituality, childhood development, nature and wildlife, and travel. I often advise authors as to the marketability of their book ideas, and I sometimes project manage books from start to finish.

As an editor/book doctor, I have helped my clients produce books worthy of numerous awards. Two such books were finalists in awards sponsored by *USA Today* and another won the Grand Prize in the Best Beach Books Festival in 2009, which culminated in an awards banquet at the famed Algonquin Hotel in New York. Two of my edited titles which were self-published were purchased and published by Macmillan in seven Asian countries.

As a journalist and travel writer, I have written articles for such publications as *Woman's Day, Travel Savvy, Medical Economics, South China Morning Post,* and others. As a copywriter, I have written speeches, website copy, whitepapers, newsletters, press releases, brochures, case studies, and a host of other marketing materials. This has included the ghostwriting of promotional materials for books.

I'm a member of the Authors Guild and two travel writer associations, as well as the Association of Ghostwriters. I'm also a published nature/wildlife photographer, professional speaker, published poet and fiction writer, and a magna cum laude college graduate with a B.A. in English. Please visit my websites for more information about me at www.facebook.com/l/369cde-iui4NJUUQWWq-yH4hmJQ; www.RuletheWord.com and www.facebook.com/l/369cddTuQwmBvrAG520KwJWEPvg; www.BestGhostwritersForHire.com, and feel free to give me a call at [number omitted] to discuss how a book can take your career to the next level.

Sincerely,
Melanie Votaw

Chapter 5

Ghost-Hunting: Finding Work Online

As a ghost, you may be lucky enough to get referrals or leads from other writers, editors, and colleagues. In addition to pursuing those potential clients, I suggest you troll for potential ghosting gigs online, on sites including: You can also find potential ghosting gigs at websites including:

- www.gorkanajobs.com
- www.journalismjobs.com
- www.online-writing-jobs.com
- www.freelancewritinggigs.com
- www.problogger.com
- www.freelancewritinggigs.com
- www.craiglist.org
- www.mediabistro.com

Keep in mind that ghosting work isn't always called that in job listings. Terms like "content marketing," "guest blogging," "copywriting," or "web copy" are often code for ghosting in that you're expected to write in the voice of your client and work without a byline.

"Many jobs listed on the job boards for copywriters are actually for content marketing writers," says Jennifer Goforth Gregory. "Since the field of content marketing is still evolving, both writers and brands are confused about the difference and exactly what skill sets brands need from writers to produce effective copy. There are definitely a lot of similarities between the two types of writing and most every successful copywriter can easily transition into content marketing writing, but there are subtle differences between the two types of writing.

"On the other hand, the purpose of content marketing writing is to inform and educate the customer on topics that the brand's customers care about," she adds. "Effectively content marketing does not include a call to action or overly 'salesy' language. The writing is typically in the style that you would see in consumer or trade publications, often includes expert sources and usually does not mention specific company products."

No matter what it's called, there is plenty of ghosting work to be found online. However, you have to know how to decipher the ads to determine which have potential and which aren't worth your time. You don't want to waste hours reading through material only to discover they have no budget for a book project, or exchange lengthy emails with someone who's never going to commit to going forward with their blog project.

When you're looking at posts or ads looking for a ghostwriter, consider the following questions:

- What type of work is the potential client looking for? How is the work described?
- Is the potential client looking for writers with a certain level of experience or knowledge about the subject matter? (Ads that say something like, "perfect for students" or "no experience necessary" usually pay nothing—or offer you "exposure" for your work.)
- Does the ad mention pay? (If not, huge red flag.) If it does specify pay, is the pay reasonable for the type of work involved?
- How well is the ad written? My experience has taught me that misspellings and grammatical errors = waste of time.

To help you distinguish between ads of promise, and those that aren't worth your time, let's take a closer look at some actual posts [all identifying information has been redacted]. We'll start with shorter types of work and then move into ads that are looking for ghostwriters for books. After each ad, you'll find my comments about its potential in brackets.

Freelance writer for health and wellness blog

We're looking for a freelance writer to regularly contribute health and lifestyle content for a consumer-focused wellness blog. Topics will cover healthy eating, fitness and exercise, general lifestyle tips. Ideally you have demonstrated online expertise and authority in the field of health and wellness in the past. We want someone who can motivate and engage our audience while giving them information and resources that help them to live healthier.

Requirements:

- Craft exceptional written materials that are clear, concise and punchy
- Quickly deliver on content requests with tight deadlines
- Adapt yourself to different content writing requests
- Speak confidently and expertly on all topics of health and wellness
- Strike a balance between motivational and informational, with a touch of humor

About you:

- Registered nurse or medical professional background preferred
- You have an entertaining, consumer-friendly writing style
- You have a strong attention to detail and mastery of grammar
- You are highly creative, witty and flexible
- You are passionate about health and wellness
- You are able to do extra research when needed
- You have a basic familiarity with SEO best practices

Please include an online portfolio or samples of your previous work along with your resume.

This is a freelance gig with ongoing content needs. The right candidate with great writing skills, health fluency and an ability to meet deadlines will be in a position to take advantage of our growing content opportunities.

[To me, this ad has promise. I wish it mentioned pay, but it appears to be a legitimate opportunity, especially if you have the medical background the company's looking for.]

Aspiring Journalist to Ghostwrite Insightful Articles on TAX blog

We are looking for a tax expert writer to ghostwrite daily a blog about emerging tax issues and opportunities for corporations and HNW individuals. Focus is on California but discussion of federal tax and international tax shelter planning and other complex issues as well. If you have tax background and would be interested please write in and tell us a bit about yourself and please suggest 3 to 5 topics which you would be interested to write your first article about if hired. Thank you!

Pay is $50 per blog, 5 times per week for a total of $250/wk. Thank you!

[The word "aspiring" as in "aspiring journalist" is a red flag to me, and $50/post is low for this kind of work. But if you have a tax background, it might be worth contacting the company to see if it has some flexibility in its budget.]

Ghost Writer Wanted

Financial Professional looking for a ghost writer to help with various ideas and articles surrounding the financial services industry. We submit articles that range from 500 words to 750 words. I am continually asked to write articles for 2-3 different industry publications and considered an expert in our field.

$0.03 per word on articles written by me but edited and expanded by you

$0.06 per word on articles developed and written by you

Compensation is paid only on articles that get published.

[You can tell this is a waste of time. First off, do the math. At $0.03/word, a 500-word post is worth a whopping $15. This person may be an expert in his field, but he's too cheap. And only paying for articles that are published? That's another red flag to me—after all, I can control the quality of my work but I can't control whether my client chooses to publish it. No thanks!]

Privacy/Tech Legal Blogger (Anywhere)

Looking for a ghost writer to regularly write articles about tech legal subjects and in particular privacy issues in the digital space.

Would prefer experience, but reliability is more important than experience. An interest in the digital/privacy space (think data breaches, legal changes, etc.) is helpful.

Please know the English language well, although sarcasm, wit, and a bit of panache is definitely acceptable.

Compensation will be per post, with a minimum quality/word count.

Legal analysis not necessary.

Please forward any relevant experience, a short statement about your interest in the industry/area, and desired compensation per post.

[This ad may have promise. No, it doesn't mention pay, but if you have experience in the area, it would be worth pursuing.]

Online Freelance Content Writers

A fast-paced New York-based company is seeking freelance writers with previous online writing experience in their area of expertise. We are looking for freelancers who can produce high quality, well-researched, and engaging work. The subject matter of articles may include medical, health, science, fitness, nutrition and environmental topics. The freelancers we seek will be highly skilled, self-motivated and experienced web writers with a deep passion for their topic area and will possess impeccable journalistic integrity. Most projects will be assigned, but our writers are encouraged to propose content that meets the diverse, everyday needs of our readers. Writers will be able to manage their own schedules and hours, and will have the opportunity to produce content on a regular basis.

Two+ years of copywriting experience required.

BA in journalism preferred.

Writing assignments start at $20-$30 per 300- to 500-word article, payable on acceptance.

If interested, please forward your resume and two published writing samples demonstrating your ability to thoroughly research topics and write concisely.

[Yes, the ad requests writers with experience who can produce "high-quality, well-researched, and engaging work. Yet its rates are low—

$20-30/post. But you know what? I might pursue this opportunity to see how the company is willing to pay writers. It might be worth sending a quick LOI.]

Experienced Freelance Writers Needed

An inbound marketing agency is looking for experienced freelance writers to create blogs on a variety of technology and business topics. This weekly position is about five hours of work a week with a 60-minute training session. Compensation varies by type of content.

We're looking for writers in a number of business and technology areas, including:

1) Oil and gas/energy: We're looking for an experienced writer with at least 3 years of experience covering the oil and gas/energy industry. Familiarity with IT and other technology topics is a plus.

2) Business intelligence: We're looking for writers that are familiar with a variety of business intelligence solutions, including IBM and SAP.

If interested, please send a resume and three recent clips.

[Here's another ghostwriting gig that doesn't say "ghostwriting." No pay is mentioned, but as an agency, it's safe to assume it will pay bloggers—hopefully well—for their work.]

Fashion Experts/Bloggers

We are premier Plus size fashion discovery website.[stet] We are looking for plus size fashion experts and bloggers. This is an impactful and visible role. This is a fun job with a good pay !!! [stet] Please send link to your blog, social media sites, websites where we can see your work, fans, followers. We look forward to hearing from you.

Qualifications:

- Deep knowledge of the plus size women (age 18-34 & 35-55) market.

- Deep understanding of pain points and needs of fashion

loving plus size women
- Active in social media like (Facebook, Twitter, Pinterest, Instagram)
- Good knowledge of their buying behaviour and factors that impact their buying.
- Deep knowledge of retailers from where they buy (e.g Torrid, Avenue, Lane Bryant, etc.)
- Good fashion choice that is trendy, fashionable that these women will love.
- Good writing skills
- Good communication skills.

Pay is negotiable and commensurate with experience and skills

[As with many blogging gigs, you're expected to have a social media presence for this job. The way this job post is written, though, I'd say it has promise—and if I met the qualifications, I would definitely send an LOI.]

Completely New And Original Healthcare Content Needed (NYC)

We're a primary care doctor's office in Brooklyn and we have lots of great pages about our services but we don't have many links because we haven't yet produced original, interesting healthcare-related content.

If you have a background in healthcare and you have something completely new and original in mind which you could ghostwrite for us, please get in touch. Our primary clientele is people from the Caribbean (East Flatbush, Flatlands, etc.) but it might not really be possible to incorporate that. Maybe you're a well-regarded author or professor and you can ghostwrite or co-author posts on our blog that will get attention. Maybe you're an expert on Caribbean, Jewish, Native American, Russian, Irish or Italian folk medicine. Maybe you're a great storyteller and your stories have been widely recognized and are highly popular. We're open to all kinds of cool ideas, as long as they are completely unique and original.

To apply, please email us with what you would like to do, what you expect to be paid and what is your basis to call yourself an expert in whatever it is you propose to write

about. If you have a resume that would be helpful too. Thank
you!

[I like the detail in this job post. I wish it mentioned specific pay, but
it does indicate that the office intends to pay contributors. That's a good
sign.]

Posts Seeking Book Ghostwriters

We've looked at ads for shorter projects; now let's look at ads seeking
ghosts for book projects. Once again, you'll find the actual job posting,
followed by comments in brackets:

Ghostwriter Needed

I'm seeking a ghostwriter to finish my book. I can afford
to pay $0.02 a word I know it's low but times are tight! The
story is based in the 50s-60s around a corrupt Irish family
outside of Boston. Send me an email if your interested.

[So, if the book winds up coming in at 70,000 words, you're looking
at $1,400. Hmmm…sounds like a good way to go broke. But maybe you
can teach your client the difference between your and you're. (I'm an apos-
trophe snob.)]

A Female Ghost Writer Needed!

You must be good in English reading and writing.
You must very open minded person. No Bible Folks!
Your age must be between 27 and 35!
Able to write Scripts for R Rated movies!
Where as many Love stories involve.
English major is a plus.
Must be able to use Laptop computers.
Flexible hours to work.
Specially Weekend or in the evening hours are available
as well."

[I'm pretty sure this person isn't a native English speaker, but this ad
scares me…I'm surprised it didn't request a recent photo and your bra size.
While I'm open-minded (and even know how to use a laptop! Go me!), I
think I'll give this one a pass. Another big clue? Absolutely no mention of
compensation. I guess writing those love stories is payment enough, right?]

Experienced Writer Needed

National motivational speaker seeking experienced writer to co-write/ghost write a motivational book. Experienced writers should be able to take my concept, story and motivational thoughts and turn them into a well written motivational guide. Please submit resume or list of other publications written.

[This ad actually may have some promise. The author said "compensation depends on experience." I'd reply to this one; I still need to know more about his project (and discuss budget, timeframe, and the like) before I say yes, but it could turn into work.]

Seeking Children's Writer

Ghostwriter wanted for children's book publishing company. Anti-bully book needed for grades 2 to 5. 24 short pages. Flat rate of $1,000 or 10% of all sales with no advance."

[Is this book worth it? It depends on the author. If you can write the book fairly quickly, $1,000 isn't a bad fee. And this job could lead to other work for the publisher. I'd pursue this one!]

Writer with Financial Experience

Nationally-known Wealth Manager based in Seattle seeks a finance-oriented writer/editor/collaborator for his John Wiley book project. Author currently has publishing deal, but requires experienced writer to polish his ideas and complement his points with research and factual background information.

This is an excellent opportunity for a budding financial writer to gain exposure in finance journalism. Through John Wiley's distribution network, this book will be in stores like Barnes and Noble, Borders and most everywhere financial books are sold. This is NOT some hokey self-publishing situation, and therefore we need a serious writer who wants to be a part of a potentially career-making book.

You will be given front-cover credit for your work, and $2500 upon manuscript acceptance by the publisher.

You must be knowledgeable about the Federal Reserve

(policies and history), foreign exchange markets, the euro-zone, global trade and fiat currencies. You will also be expected to be conversant on current financial topics such as those making headlines in major financial newspapers.

To be considered for this position, please send at least two writing samples, each covering financial market topics (i.e., topics relevant to Wall Street). Preferably, your work has been published, though we are considering a wide range of experiences for this role. Due to the significant amount of face time the author requires, we are only considering local candidates (Seattle, Portland and Vancouver).

[This is an interesting ad. While $2,500 is pretty low for the amount of work this project seems to entail, if I were a financial writer, I'd probably send an LOI and see if I could negotiate for more money. I've done this successfully with other jobs—once the client wants you, budgets can become more flexible.]

Writer Wanted

Wanted a writer for a book that's going to published and sold via infomercials. Will get a percentage of sales, plus an hourly rate will be negotiated. Must be able to work hand and hand with me and put my thoughts down on paper.

First Chance to be on the ground floor of a published book that ever city is going to see in the United States as well as Canada.

Target book sales at a low end will be 700,000. First time writers are welcome.

[So many red flags here. At the low end, this book is going to sell 700,000 copies? We're talking *Harry Potter* territory—yet first-time writers are welcome. (That's code for "we're not paying much…or anything.") And with all the hand-holding, how will I actually get the client's thoughts down?]

Writer for Book Project

Collaborating Writer needed for new book project must have past experience, nationally or locally should have credentials and referrals, e-mail for more information!

[I don't like exclamation points in job ads, but at least the client is asking for experience, credentials, and referrals—I assume he means references. On a slow day, I'd send a quick LOI; it could turn into something.]

Writer for Book Needed

I have a unique and drama filled life story that I think will interest others, unfortunately I am not a writer. The story is about my life as an adopted child and the reuniting with my biological families. You may think the story is over but not even close.

[At this point, you know to keep reading, right?]

Ghost writer to shadow physician and pen medical manual

Looking for a creative and intelligent writer to ghost write a Medical Weight Loss Program Manual. You will shadow a prominent physician for 4-6 weeks (hours are flexible) and transcribe his practice procedures, methods, techniques and idiosyncrasies, and adapt these transcriptions into a structured and comprehensive guidebook for his Weight Loss Program.

Requirements:

- Extraordinary written skills, including editing, grammar and formatting
- Keen observation skills and attention to detail
- Bachelor's degree in English, journalism or communications a plus

Rate of pay:
$12-$15/hour

[This isn't a ghostwriting job—it's a secretarial one. If you want to spend your time transcribing and make up to $15/hour doing so, it might be right for you. But I would want significantly more for this time of time commitment. And ghostwriting a book involves a lot more than "adapting transcriptions." I wouldn't pursue this gig but a less experienced ghostwriter might—and that's okay.]

Writer for E-Book

I am looking for a Writer to write an e-Book on making money with Twitter.

Pay is $100 for the entire project and I need to get rights to the e-book.

I don't have requirements on the size and length of the e-Book. I am more interested in the quality of the content.

[Interested in the quality of the content, yet only offering $100. You get what you pay for…]

Talking Work (and Even Money) with Potential Clients

I'm sure even this brief intro has given you an idea of what to look for—and what to avoid—when reading job postings. But regardless of whether you reply to an advertisement, send an LOI to someone you've heard is looking for a ghostwriter, or respond to someone who's contacted you, you have to be able to determine, fairly quickly, whether this person is a potential client. That means getting more information about the project, and the budget for same. That's what we'll cover in the next chapter.

Chapter 6

Talking Money:
What to Charge for Ghosting Gigs

Okay, you've got a lead, you've spoken with the potential client, and you want the work. What's next? Talking money.

With shorter pieces, the client may make you an offer for the work (say, $150 for a 500-word blog post, or $0.25/word for an article for a trade magazine). Or he may ask that you make a bid. (We'll talk about bidding on bigger projects in a bit.)

Keep in mind that even when a client makes you an offer, you can always *try* to get more money even with a predetermined fee, citing reasons like a tight deadline, extensive research, or a client who will be hard to reach or work with. It doesn't hurt to ask—I've never lost a potential gig by asking if there's some wiggle room in the budget. If not, you're back to square one and have to decide whether to say "yes" to the work.

As a freelancer, even before I started ghostwriting, I applied a four-part test to determine whether I took on work:

1. How much money does it pay? This is the easy part.
2. How much time will it take? Years of experience have taught me that the articles I do for national magazines takes far more time (including the pitching and follow-ups) than the work I do for smaller publications. While the big magazines pay more per word, the smaller magazines often pay more per hour because there are fewer hassles and less overall time involved.
3. What's the PIA factor? You remember what PIA stands for. Some clients and editors are just...annoying. I'm thinking of an editor I work with who takes forever to respond to

queries, then assigns stuff with ridiculously tight deadlines. I love her, but there's definitely a PIA factor involved when I write for her magazine. And if I sense that the PIA factor on a particular project may be high, I'm either going to get more money...or I might even walk away.

4. Will this work further my career—and if so, how? So, for example, way back in 2000 when I wrote my first book, *Ready, Aim, Specialize! Create your own Writing Specialty and Make More Money*, I received an advance of $2,500. And I interviewed 56 people for it! My hourly rate was close to minimum wage. But I wanted to start writing books, and I had to begin somewhere. So I said yes to the book, added "author" to my CV, and even made royalties from it. My first book led to others, which made that pathetic advance worth it.

Keep these four factors in mind as you determine whether you want a project and what to charge for it. How much you charge, and how (i.e. by the hour, by the project, by the page) will depend on the project, your client, and your own expertise.

Most clients for shorter ghosting work expect to pay either per-word or per-piece, such as with blog posts although a few may ask for an hourly rate. So what are the going rates for this kind of work? And what should you charge?

"Although, less background work (research, interviewing, etc.) is needed for ghostwriting overall, there is more attention needed to learn a specific industry, learn the client's voice and understand what they want to say, and how they want to say it," says Jill Russell Qualizza. "I base my estimates by the hour (including any basic research, interview time, writing and editing)."

Typical hourly rates for ghosts start at $25/hour and go up to more than $100/hour, depending on the type of work you're doing and the client you're working for. If you prefer to charge per-word, I suggest charging at least $0.50/word; most experienced ghostwriters charge at least $1-2/word for shorter pieces.

Bidding on Book Projects

Some clients like book packagers will tell you what they've budgeted and it's nonnegotiable. You either say "yes" or "no". It may not offer as much flexibility but it's a lot easier than bidding a job.

Once again, you can use the four-part test to determine whether you want the project:

1. How much money does it pay? This is the easy part.
2. How much time will it take? A ghostwritten book might involve expanding an already-written manuscript (which shouldn't take too long—possibly a month or two) or researching and writing the book from scratch, which typically takes at least six months. There's a big difference between the two!
3. What's the PIA factor? You can't always determine this at the outset of a book project. But if you sense that the client may be a high-maintenance one based on your early exchanges, or if the book requires a quick turnaround or a lot of extra legwork (like tracking down and interviewing sources), you'll want to be paid extra for that.
4. Will this work further my career—and if so, how? If you haven't ghostwritten a book (yet), that first ghosting gig is essential. So you may be willing to take a lower rate than a more established ghost.

Experienced ghostwriters with in-demand specialties (writing corporate histories or business books for big names, for example) can and do charge more than those who are newer to the field. "I can say that my business is up overall [compared to 2010]," says Ellen Neuborne, who's been ghostwriting for a decade. "Generally, I am able to be choosier about the clients I take…I have raised my rates, but I've done that because my experience level has gone up and so I can command a higher price."

"I think there are plenty of opportunities out there, even more than in the past. The challenge is that, in our global economy, rates are being pushed down, making it particularly difficult for those starting out," says Graciela Showalter. "New ghostwriters have to determine what rates they're willing to work for and stick to those rates. Once ghostwriters become more established, there is plenty of work out there at good living wages in everything from writing manuscripts to running blogs and social media pages, to writing speeches for company executives. The market is strong."

So, what are ghosts and coauthors getting paid today? Polling several dozen collaborators in 2013 produced the following average fee ranges:

- Book proposal, $3,500 to $10,000+.
- Book (average length 50,000-75,000 words), $7,500-

$50,000+ (most common, $15,000-$30,000).
- Consulting, $100-$300/hour.
- Corporate history, $35,000-$150,000.
- Editing/rewriting, $35-$100/hour.
- Ghostwriting, $25-$250/hour (upper range tends to be working for high-level business execs)

Even though I usually have an idea of what to charge, I *hate* quoting fees. I'm always afraid that I'm either going to charge too little and get the project (only to discover my hourly rate has bottomed out) or charge too much and lose the project to a cheaper writer. I rarely feel like I'm hitting the bidding sweet spot, but the more books and other big projects I do for clients, the better I get at estimating appropriate fees.

Before you bid, clarify the scope of the project. Will you be writing a book proposal of about 30-50 pages? A 40,000-word manuscript? Rewriting a 75,000-word memoir? You need to know about how long the book will be before you can estimate the work involved. If your client isn't sure, suggest that he find books that are similar in length to what he's envisioning; on average, a printed book contains between 300 and 400 words/page.

Second, how many of the elements are you responsible for? Are you writing an introduction in addition to chapters? Does he expect you to provide a bibliography or index? (I'm willing to help with a bibliography, but I don't provide indexing services. Other ghosts may.) Does your client want or expect you to write the cover copy for the book itself? It's better to ask now than be surprised in the future.

Third, how will you be working? Are you writing from scratch or does the client have an outline you'll follow? Has he started a draft? Will you interview him, or other sources, or both? Will you be responsible for all writing, with your client signing off, or will he be writing some, or any, of the book himself? Will you be doing research on your own? Will you have to meet with your client, or travel, and if so, how much? You've got to know *what* you're bidding on to determine how much you'll charge.

That's why I typically ask questions like the following:

- What kind of book (or other project) do you have in mind? (Is it a memoir, a business book, a how-to, a children's book? In other words, what is her book about?)
- *Why* do you want to write this book? Is there more than one reason? (For example, does she want to capture her family's

history? Does she want to attract more clients to her business? Is her goal to make money from the book or is it more important to simply see it in print?)

- What kind of material do you have to draw from? Do you already have the book started, or other research or resources I can use? Do you have an outline? Do you know how long the book will be? (Sometimes clients will have a draft, or some chapters, or rough notes and research you can use. Sometimes they will have an outline they want you to follow. Sometimes they will have nothing—the book is all in their head. That's fine, but more work for you in the long run.)

- What kind of timeline are you envisioning? Do you want to get started right away? When do you want to have the book in print?

- Why are you considering using a ghostwriter or coauthor for your book? Do you have a preference? (You may have to explain the difference here. Many clients want you to remain invisible, and insist that you work as a ghost. Others may be fine with a coauthor credit. It doesn't matter to me, though I usually charge a little more for ghosting gigs.)

- Have you worked with a ghost or writer in the past? How did that work out?

- What kind of publisher do you plan to work with? Are you planning to try to sell your book to a traditional publisher or publish it with a POD publisher? (This is an important question as you may have to explain the difference between publishing options to potential clients. We'll talk more about that later in chapter five.)

- Do you have an intended audience in mind for this book? Who will your readers be? Why will they buy your book? (This latter question may be moot if the person simply wants to publish a book for friends and family, but any author who wants to actually sell books must understand that people have to have a need for his book before they'll shell out money for it.)

- Have you thought about how you'd like to work with a writer? (We'll talk more about this in the next chapter, but does the client have a draft that he wants help with? Does he want you to interview him and write the book following a format he's come up with? Or are you starting from scratch?)

- What budget do you have in mind for this book? (We've arrived at money at last.) Here's where I've had would-be clients say something like, "but I thought you got paid when the book becomes a best-seller," or "well, I hadn't really thought about that," or "I can't afford to spend much."

That may be the case, but I want to know that now, before I invest any more time and effort—say, reading through their material or giving them more publishing advice—at this point. It may sound harsh, but my work time is limited. If the person hedges on budget, I'll say something like, "for typical ghosting projects, I charge between $20,000 and $30,000 but that depends on a lot of factors. If you have a book that needs editing or you're going to do a lot of the writing yourself, I charge less, but again, each project is different. Once I know more about what your goals are, what you have to work with in terms of material and research, and how we'd be working together, I'd be happy to give you a bid of what I'd charge for the project.")

Talk to any experienced ghostwriter and they all say the same thing—to avoid wasting time, they bring up money pretty quickly. After all, our most valuable asset as self-employed writers is our time. If we don't make the most of it, we can't make a decent living.

"I try to bring it up early as possible without sounding really obnoxious," says Marcia Layton Turner. "Early in my career I could have two long phone conversations talking about the book before we talked money, but now I try to bring it up early as possible. Often it's in an email—'what's your budget? What are you expecting to pay for it? How will the money work? Have you been offered an advance?'"

The type of client you're pitching makes a difference, too. The Everyday Joe, or EJ, typically doesn't ask about rates—he may even assume you'll work for a share of the profits. (It's up to you to set him straight.) Pros with a platform (PPs), agents, and corporate clients are more likely to ask about rates. And with book publishers or packagers, the client may tell you the budget for the project—and then you can take it or walk away.

"Often the client brings it up first, with a 'how much do you charge' type of question. Because my clients are generally in the business world, this isn't as awkward as it might be with other types of clients," says Jacqueline Lynn. "Sometimes I tell a story of a woman who I met years ago at a writers' event who was raving about how much she loved to write and she would do it if she didn't get paid. My comment was, 'I love what I do, but I do it for the money.' This gets a laugh, but it makes my point. I'm a professional and I get paid like one."

To avoid spending time with clients who can't (or won't) pay, Jill Amadio's website includes her rates. "I post my prices on my site in order to save time and screen out those who are not serious potential clients," says Amadio. "The pricing lets them know right away if they can afford to finance the project or not, and what is involved."

Of course your initial conversation with a potential client isn't only about money. Take careful notes and listen, really listen to this person. Does the subject of the book interest you? Do you think you could write it? Do you *want* to write it? Are you and this person "clicking"? Does she sound like someone you could spend months working with? Is she appreciative of the questions you're asking and the knowledge (for example, the difference in publishing options) you're sharing with her? Does she respect your expertise and ability? Often you'll know in the first conversation if this is someone you can work well with—and I suggest you trust your gut.

If your prospect is approaching this book as a way to make money (as opposed to getting a family history in print, for example), you may have to set him straight about the work and time involved to actually sell the book after it's published. "Most of the books I do are self-published and the people I work with are speakers or doctors, and they have an audience," says Melanie Votaw. "I discourage people otherwise—they have no idea of what it's going to be like for them to sell a book if they have nothing set up. I feel like I'm smashing their dreams a lot of the time, but it's better to do that than have them be thousands of dollars in the hole and be unable to sell the book." If you're an author yourself, you already know that even with a traditional publisher, the burden of selling the published book falls on the author's shoulders.

Advances and Royalties, and How to Split Them

There's another issue to consider if you're writing a book which will be traditionally published, and that's the matter of the advance, and potential royalties. I say potential royalties for a reason—recall from chapter 1 that most books do not "earn out," or pay royalties. The advance you receive may well be the only money you (or your client) ever sees from your work.

So how much of the advance do you get to keep? What percentage of the royalties, if any, do you receive? Remember too that unless your client already has a book deal in hand, you cannot guarantee a certain advance. So if the book fails to command the advance you want, is the client willing to pay the difference?

"In most cases I'm going to ask for 100 percent of the advance if I'm setting aside my time to produce this project," says Turner. "That's what the advance money is for—for my time. The author [client] is going to put in a little bit of time, but they don't always have the time or talent to do it. That's what the advance is meant for—the time to write the book."

An advance is actually an "advance against royalties," the amount the author makes on the books that are sold. So what happens with royalties (assuming the book makes them)? Will you get a percentage of the royalties or are you doing the book for a flat fee? I suggest that you try to get royalties on the back end—they can be a source of income for years as long as the book stays in print. Stephanie Golden is still making royalties on a book she coauthored ten years ago!

Often if the ghostwriter gets more than half of the advance, the author/client receives all of the royalties until an agreed percentage is reached. So, for example, for a recent project, I was paid $5,000 for a book proposal and $10,000 for the manuscript itself. My agreement with the client provides that she'll receive the first $15,000 in royalties (so she makes up what she put into the book) and then we go 50/50 after that.

Tim Gower worked with a client where they had agreed how to divide the advance in terms of percentages. "What happened was that we didn't get the advance we wanted—it was considerably smaller than what we wanted," says Gower. "The advance ended up being just enough for me to live on for a year, so I got 100 percent of it."

Gower was lucky that his coauthor agreed to this split—that doesn't always happen. "I generally put a clause in the contract that says the amount that I'll be paid," says Golden. "If the advance doesn't pay that amount, then the other person can renegotiate and pay the rest out of their pocket."

If you don't get the advance you want, don't be sucked in to doing a book for the royalties. No matter how much blockbuster potential a book has, there are no guarantees—and you don't want to spend months of your life working for free, or close to it. "You have to be paid, and you have to be paid up front, and you have to make sure that you're paid with enough income to adequately compensate you before you even *think* about what the book is going to bring in [in royalties]," says Golden. "You cannot depend on the book bringing in money to pay you afterwards."

Talking Covers and Credit

I already mentioned the difference between ghostwriting and coauthoring; with the latter, the writer's name appears on the book's cover, with an "and" or "with," as in "by Celebrity with Wonderful Coauthor," or "by Medical Expert and Talented Coauthor."

Does it matter whether you're a ghost or coauthor? That's up to you. I've worked with clients who were willing to coauthor and share credit (although they owned the copyright to the work) and I've worked with clients where I wrote the book as a true ghost. If your client insists that you ghost, you have to balance how much it matters to you and your career not to have your name on the book.

For example, my first book collaboration, *Small Changes, Big Results* (written with Ellie Krieger, R.D., a well-known dietitian), has sold quite well. My name's on the cover (albeit in much smaller type) and that fact alone has led to at least five ghosting and coauthoring projects. The book itself has become a marketing tool for me.

I will say that if I think a book will sell well and boost my own platform, I'm going to try to work as a coauthor, not a ghost. My name on the cover may mean more projects for me down the road, after all. So I usually take the approach that I want cover credit, and use that at a negotiating point if the client insists on a ghostwriter. In other words, I'm willing to ghost instead of coauthor—but I'm going to ask for more money if I'm not going to be named.

Editor-turned-freelancer Sondra Forsyth has always shared credit on her coauthored books. "I like to keep my name out there!" says Forsyth, author/coauthor of eleven books published by top houses. "The flip side is that because of my connections in the publishing world and good reviews for my previous books, my co-authors find that my name adds value."

Some projects, like celebrity bios, are almost always ghostwritten. Others may be ghosted or coauthored. "I'm credited on all of my corporate and organizational histories," says Kathi Ann Brown. "The only corporate book for which I didn't get 'full' credit is the one I co-wrote with J. W. Marriott, Jr., Chairman of Marriott International. We share equal credit. One of my family histories was also a 'co-author' scenario. I did all the research and writing but one of the family members was responsible for corralling more than 100 of her relatives to participate. She definitely earned equal credit—in fact, I think maybe she had the harder job of the two of us!"

One more thing about ghostwriting versus coauthoring—whether you get credit has nothing to do with how you're paid. In other words, many ghostwriting gigs are for a flat fee, but you can sometimes negotiate royalties if your client sells his book to a traditional publisher. And even if you're listed as a coauthor, you may do a book for a set fee. Don't assume that coauthors always share in royalties, or that ghosts can't get them.

What About the Editor?

If you are working for a client who plans to self-publish using a POD company, your job is to make him happy. When you work for a client who has a traditional publishing contract, though—or will have one—you need to clarify a couple of points.

First, who will the contact person be? When I've worked with clients with traditional deals, my client has always been the "point person" as far as the editor goes. She is the one who communicates with the editor, turns in chapters, and handles revision requests (even though I'm probably the one doing all of the revising). However, this is entirely up to the client and ghost.

The question of edits is an important one, too. It's safe to assume that even if you write a book that pleases your client—the author—her *editor* will request changes and rewrites. These may be minimal or more significant, so factor that into account before you sign a client. Once those edits are completed, and the book is in the final galleys phase, it should be your client's responsibility to read them over for the final proof. But what if your client thinks it's your job? Make sure that details like these are addressed in your contract so there are no misunderstandings down the line. [We'll talk more about ghostwriting contracts in chapter 7.]

Another question is whether you'll actually be a signatory to the contract between the publisher and the author. In some cases, the publisher wants you to sign the publishing contract; in others, the client/author signs the contract with the publisher and you have a stand-alone agreement with the client to actually write the book. In that case, it's wise to make sure the publisher has already approved you as the ghost.

Listen to your Gut

After considering all the above, there's one more factor to consider—that "still, small voice" every writer has. Does the project feel right to you? Are you excited about taking it on? Or are you overlooking some red flags because your bank balance is low, or thinking, "this client sounds like a jerk, but I really need the money?" If so, tread carefully.

Over the years, I've noticed that PIA clients almost always exhibit signs early on that warn they're going to be, um, *challenging* to deal with. The following are all red flags that a potential client may not be worth your time:

- Potential client insists book will be a bestseller (or wants you to guarantee same).

- Potential client uses phrases like "shocking cover-up, "once-in-a-lifetime story," "plenty of people want me dead," "you'll never believe that this really happened," etc.
- Potential client refuses to talk money upfront.
- Potential client refuses to sign a written contract with you.
- Potential client misses phone calls or fails to do something (such as sending you a signed contract or check) that he said he would.
- Potential client insists that he *could* write the book, but he doesn't have the time. (Implies a lack of respect for your ability.)
- Potential client wants a writer "like Jon Krakauer or Malcolm Gladwell" or some other big name. Unless you can write like them, he's likely to be disappointed. (Usually this desire is paired with a budget of about $400.)
- Potential client doesn't have a working knowledge of technology—i.e., wants you to mail hard copies so he can edit by hand and you can "type" his changes in. If a client can't work with Word and email, I won't work with him.
- Potential client wants you to meet constantly, or spend weeks together working on the book. (I actually had a potential client who suggested we spend several weekends in a hotel room "banging out" the book. Um, I said no…my husband wouldn't have been okay with that working arrangement. On the other hand, if the client's willing to pay for it, I'm fine with face-to-face meetings, but generally it's less expensive for clients and less time-consuming for me if we work through phone and email. Clients almost always agree when I point this out.)
- Potential client doesn't know *what* he wants. Or keeps changing his mind, or waffling on going forward. If he's waffling early in the game, it will probably get worse in the future.

Gwen Moran makes sure that she and her client are a good fit for each other before she takes on a ghosting or coauthoring project. "I usually take some time getting to know the prospect and making sure we feel comfortable with each other, especially on book projects," says Moran. "They're like little marriages—you're spending a great deal of time with someone over a period of months. You have to have respect and trust each other in order to move forward. Before I sign anything, I want to make sure we have similar work styles and expectations, so I explain how I prefer to work, the levels of flexibility I have, and what my boundaries are."

And if something feels wrong—or it sounds too good to be true—don't be afraid to say no. "My best advice is to go with your gut. If you feel like there are red flags and you can afford to say no, say no," says Votaw. "Nine times out of ten, your gut is right. Every time I've gone against that feeling, it's been a disaster."

Making Your Bid

Ed Robertson always prefers to review material from a potential client before he bids on a job. "I'll say, 'let me see what you have,' or ask for something to look at," says Robertson. "After I review the material, I'll come up with a couple of scenarios that will work for them and work for me. People will say, 'give me a ballpark'...but every project has a life of its own. I like to look at something first before I can make an intelligent remark on it."

Even after years in the business, Robertson finds bidding challenging. "The last couple of years, I've had to adjust my rates a little bit to be competitive but I have lost projects because I've bid too high," he says. "Everybody wants as much as they can have for as little as they can pay."

Like Robertson, Marcia Layton Turner asks specific questions before she estimates a job. "How long is the book going to be? Where is the information coming from? In some cases, I'll get nervous because all of the information is coming from the person's head. I like to have some backup, some scientific confirmation that this is the case, or that this is the smart approach to take," says Turner. "And I want to make sure that their timeline is reasonable. If they want it done by 30 days, it's not going to happen. Four months or six months is okay."

I can't overstate the importance of knowing what your client will provide you with (if anything) before you agree to do it for a set price. Years ago I agreed to ghost a book for a nonprofit organization, based on what I was told—that the organization had dozens of articles it owned the copyright to that I could use for the book. I quoted a price, the client agreed, and sent over the material. Guess what? More than 90 percent of that material wasn't owned by the organization; it was a collection of articles and research pulled from the web authored (and copyrighted) by other sources. I wound up writing the entire book from scratch, not what I'd originally envisioned. If I would have known how little material the client had for me to pull from, I would have charged at least double my original fee.

Kathi Ann Brown's first corporate history was for a client that let her charge by the hour, but her second was for a flat fee that didn't cover her time, a "typical rookie error." "Since then I've learned to ballpark a fee that I can live with, but am careful in any contract to put in clauses that make clear that the fee covers only a certain number of interviews and only one set of revisions before an hourly fee kicks in," says Brown. "Doing so helps clients think about whether every single person they want me to interview is going to be worth the extra cost. And charging for revisions beyond a first comprehensive round likewise makes 'em focus on getting all their revisions and comments to me at one time so we stay on track time-wise."

When it comes to *how* you charge for book-length projects, you have three choices:

• *By the hour.* This is actually my favorite way to charge, probably because of my former life as a lawyer. You agree to an hourly fee, you track your time, and your client pays you. "I usually work hourly, because every book is different and it's very difficult to determine how much time it's going to take," says Melanie Votaw. "If clients are squeamish about working hourly, I say, 'If I give you a flat fee, I have to pad it because that's the only way I can protect my business, and this way you'll only pay me for the work I do." Votaw takes a retainer upfront, and then sends a weekly accounting to her client so that he knows exactly how much time she's putting in. I've worked with clients where I've charged a per-hour fee with the caveat that I'll keep the total amount under a certain figure. This makes both me and the client happy.

• *By the word/by the page.* If you came to ghostwriting via magazine or newspaper freelancing, you're familiar with the per-word rate. It's less common when writing books, but some clients may ask that you charge on a per-word or per-page basis, say $25-50/page.

• *By the project.* In other words, you charge one fee that includes the entire project. Book publishers, packagers, agents, and many PPs will ask for a project fee so they know exactly what they're going to be paying. If you do charge a flat fee, make sure that you describe what the project includes (and what it does not)—such as by specifying one or two revisions, or that the client will supply you with research or access to materials you need for the book.

Jacqueline Lynn says that per-project fees work well for her and her clients. "I think it's easier for everyone if we all know exactly what the project includes and how much it's going to cost," says Lynn. "With that said, I know how much I want to make per hour, and I keep that in mind when setting a project fee. I have had clients who have put me on a retainer, but that usually doesn't happen until I've been working with them a while and we have a very strong trust factor in play and a lot of different projects in the works."

After a potential client and I have talked and I have an idea of what I'm getting into, how much work it will be, and how much time I'll invest, I make my bid in writing. In that bid, I explain the planned scope of work and what my rate will be for it. I always give a little ="wiggle room" in case the client wants to negotiate—in other words, I don't give my "bottom" number, or the least amount I'm willing to do the project for.

I suggest you provide written bids as well. Don't quote a figure off of the top of your head. Describe what you'll do, how it will benefit your client, and how much it will cost. Then give him time to digest it.

I've included three samples to give you templates to work with. Note that I provide an idea of what my plans are but I don't "give away the store" with too many specifics. That will occur once we agree on a fee, and I'm working for the client.

On the following pages you will find four actual bids that worked for me. The first was for a potential client who wanted me to write her book proposal; the second is for a book packager seeking a writer for one of its clients; the third was for an author who needed an editor for his manuscript; and the fourth was for a client who contacted me about editing his book.

Dear POTENTIAL CLIENT:

First, thanks so much for getting in touch with me earlier this week. I'm really excited about your book concept and the possibility of us working together. I think you have a lot of good ideas, and also feel that I can bring a lot to both the proposal and the book itself. (Oh, and thanks for sending the research you sent last night—I read through it and there's a lot of good stuff there as well.)

The seeds for the book are there. There's still much to do, however. Working together, we need to come up with a title and subtitle; an overview; the "hook" (i.e., what makes this book different from everything else out there);

competitive analysis (a rundown on the book's likely biggest competitors and how it's different than/better than the other titles, which relates to the hook); the audience (is it *all* career-oriented busy people, or more aimed at women or men, for example); marketing/promotion (again, you've got a platform already but we really want to showcase this in the proposal); about the author(s) (depending on whether you want to include me as coauthor in the proposal—I think that's a selling point but that's your call); the overall structure (i.e., total number of chapters, pages, appendices, and the like); the chapter summaries; and one well-written sample chapter of approximately 15 to 20 pages. The total proposal will come in at 30-40 pages.

Sound like a lot? It is. But the end product—the finished proposal—will be worth it. I'm assuming that you're willing to do some of the research and work with me on the sample chapter and overview in particular; that will save me some time. As I told you yesterday, I typically charge $5000 to $10,000 for a typical proposal, but considering the subject matter and the level of your involvement, my fee will be **$4,500**. This includes all of the elements of the proposal including one sample chapter, to be delivered within four to six weeks (at a date we agree on.) I'd like $2,000 on going forward/signing a collaboration agreement (see below); $1,000 upon delivery of the draft proposal (without the sample chapter): and $1,500 upon delivery of the finished proposal with the sample chapter.

With the polished, finished proposal in hand, you'll be ready to pitch agents and editors—and you'll have the framework for the book completed which makes the actual writing of it easier. I know you want to use the book to take the next step in your career, but I also think you have a saleable idea, a strong platform, and the dedication to see the project through—all of which is necessary to succeed as a book author!

Another thing to consider is when you want to sign a formal collaboration agreement that sets out our expectations for working together. We can sign one for the proposal itself, or for a potential book deal, or work something out that you're comfortable with. I can send you a sample one that you can tweak/modify how you see fit.

What else? I think we've got a good rapport, and I'm reliable, professional, and easy to work with. If I tell you I'm going to do something, you can count on me to get it done. I love collaborating with smart people to get their ideas in print, and helping them become book authors.

Please let me know if you have any questions about my bid or the project—I hope we'll have the chance to work together! If this is a go, I can make your proposal my first priority, and I think you (and hopefully a wonderful agent and editor as well) will be delighted with the finished product. Let me know if you're ready to take the next step.

All good things,
Kelly

[Note how I describe the many elements of book proposal in this bid; I want the client to realize that a proposal takes a lot of time to research and write. But I also describe the benefits of creating such a proposal on the top of the page to help convince her to say "yes" to this bid.]

Dear BOOK PACKAGER:

Thanks for your time on Thursday, and for giving me the opportunity to consider CLIENT's book project. I think he has some great ideas, and I'm always interested in the psychological side of things, including sales, and believe I can bring a unique perspective to this project. I've already thought of some ways we can expand the book and make it more useful in helping salespeople make changes in the way they work, such as including quizzes and other interactive pieces that engage and involve readers.

A little about me: I've been a fulltime freelancer for the last decade. Since then, more than 700 of my articles have appeared in 50 national magazines including *Redbook, Self, Health, Family Circle, Woman's Day, Continental, Fitness,* and *Shape.* I'm the coauthor of *Small Changes, Big Results: A 12-Week Action Plan to a Better Life* (with Ellie Krieger, R.D./ Random House, 2005), a nutrition/fitness/wellness book and am the author of five other books including *Six-Figure Freelancing: The Writer's Guide to Making More Money* as well as two successful novels.

In addition to writing books and articles, I've also written several book proposals, including a recent collaboration with a Ph.D. (working title, "Cell Power: The Comprehensive Program to Maintain your Cellular Health") which my agent is shopping now. Over the last decade, I've worked with hundreds of health, fitness, nutrition, and business experts on projects including articles, marketing pieces, book proposals, and books. I know how important it is to capture and reflect each expert's unique voice, and also have experience reporting and writing the "real-life" anecdotes (even if they're fictionalized) that make books and articles compelling and memorable.

As a writer, I specialize in health, wellness, psychology, fitness, and nutrition subjects, and I enjoy collaborating with experts to help them communicate their message to audiences. I've also written about business subjects ranging from marketing to motivating employees. I own BodyWise Consulting, and speak and consult about subjects ranging from time management to goal-setting to freelancing. I enjoy helping people make positive changes in their lives through my work as an author, journalist, and speaker, and it sounds like CLIENT has a similar mission in mind when it comes to salespeople.

That's why I hope CLIENT will keep me in mind for his ghost-writing project. Though the figure you mentioned ($9,000) is a bit low for what I usually charge (and for what I think I can bring to the project), I'd appreciate a chance to talk with him more if he thinks I'm a good fit for his book. I'd probably quote a figure closer to $12,000 to $15,000, and can guarantee that we'll finish the book within his time parameters. As a fellow speaker, I understand the importance of back-room sales, and I'm sure he wants to get his book in print as soon as reasonably possible!

You have samples of my work, but if you need anything else, just let me know and I'll be happy to provide it. I have a big project due February 10, but could start on his project by mid-February if he's interested in working with me. Please feel free to contact me directly or visit my website, www.becomebodywise.com, for more information about my background.

Thank you very much for your time and have a great week!

All best,
Kelly James-Enger

[The budget for this particular book was too low for me to take it on, but I wanted to be considered. Here I play up my unique experience and background and then argue that I should be paid more. It worked—not only did the client hire me, he paid me the $15,000 I asked for without batting an eye.]

Hi, Dick—

First off, you definitely have a great story! I love how you started the book—great "hook" that definitely wanted me to keep reading more. Your writing is technically fine, but I see a lot of ways to improve the story, make it more readable/of interest. Sometimes I feel like there's a little too much "engineer-speak" going on, making it drier than it should be. In my opinion, what you need isn't a ghostwriter per se so much as a developmental editor; someone who can take what you have and show you where and how it can be improved. From our conversation, it sounds like that's what you're looking for, too.

You really have two projects here—the book proposal

(if you decide you want to market it to a traditional publisher) and the book manuscript itself. Your book proposal needs some work to make it marketable; I've written/collaborated on about ten of them and have attached one so you can see what the format typically looks like. You've got some great stuff there (like your speaking gigs, published articles, publicity, etc.) but a book proposal really needs to drive home the target market for the title, how you'll SELL the book (that's all publishers care about these days!), and how, in so many words, you're going to help the publisher make money. I think if you take a look at the attached, you'll see what I mean.

The book itself would benefit from some color, rewriting to make it more "lively" and readable. I like your voice but I think you're missing some details that would make it more compelling. I have a lot of ideas that we can discuss further if we decide to work together.

With book clients, I typically charge an hourly rate as opposed to a flat project fee (unless I'm working for a book packager that uses project fees.) My rate for this kind of consulting/editing/writing work is $100/hour. I'm not cheap but I'm very good, and I can help you research and identify possible publishers, write a query letter, etc., if you want. I'm thinking it would be about 5-10 hours of work for what you've given me already, no more than 10 to give you an idea of how long things take me. (I'm a former attorney so I'm comfortable tracking my time and billing by the hour so you know how I'm spending my time.)

If that fits your budget for the project, I'd suggest meeting in person and I'll work up (i.e. mark up and make suggestions for improvement) the chapters I have and we can discuss them. Then you can write the other chapters as you're going along and I can edit/work up and/or work on the proposal/research publishers/whatever you like. Basically my role is to help you make the book as good as you can, and hopefully sell it to a publisher as well.

What else can I tell you? I enjoy collaborating with fellow authors and am easy to work with. I'm direct and will tell you if I think something should be changed (and why), but the bottom line is that it is *your* book and I always recognize and respect that. My work as a writer and speaker involves sharing information with readers and listeners to help them change their lives for the better, so I definitely think I'd be a good fit for you! I'm happy to answer any questions about the process, etc.; just let me know.

Thanks for thinking of me and considering me for this project, and I look forward to hearing from you soon.

All my best,
Kelly

[Notice that I explain that what the client needs is actually two different projects—a book proposal and the book itself. I wasn't sure of how long editing the book would take, so I quoted an hourly fee instead of a project fee here.]

Hey, Jon!

Hope you had a great weekend, first off. Thanks for giving me the opportunity to read through/review your book. I'm thinking you don't need an edit—you need a reworking of the book itself.

Here's what I'm thinking—I would completely reorganize the material for the book (cutting the majority of chaps 1-3) and rework it to be more of a guide for personal trainers. You make that promise, but it's not really coming through...your message is diluted (in my opinion) by getting too deeply into your real-life anecdotes/asides without giving your readers a real "plan" to become more successful. I would also include more valuable information (for example, giving a rundown of different certification organizations, costs, pros and cons of each) than telling them to research them on their own.

Another example—you tell readers to go to the gym and find mentors. My thought was, 1. That's not helpful. 2. How do they know **who** should be their mentors? You could include a section on how to choose a mentor, what to look for, etc. And you don't want to keep pointing readers to your website; they should get the info they need from the book itself. That's a big turnoff for readers.

Bottom line is that you have some good ideas here (aha moments, creating emotional involvement, focus system, etc.) but I think that's getting lost in the not-so-great stuff. And there's a lot of that...like going on and on about *Rich Dad/Poor Dad* without giving readers a lot of actionable steps about how they can save money, make more, etc.

Here's what I'd suggest. If you're interested in hiring me to rework the framework of the book, that will give you a guideline/formula to follow (and I'll note where I think you should add more material, etc.) as you rework the manuscript. It will be more reader-friendly and much more helpful—and if you decide you want me to stay on as an editor/ghost/etc., I'll consider that, too, although I think with guidance you can write a lot of it yourself. I see this as two separate projects, though and suggest you start with the first one—to completely rework the book's framework and structure it to deliver on your title's promise.

I'd charge **$2,000** to create an entirely new outline for the book, including incorporating existing material and telling you what is missing/what needs to be added. This may sound like a lot but what I can do for you is create the entire framework for the next step—adding material where necessary, etc.—and if you want, we can go from there to finish the book. I do think the first step is essential though because the material lacks overall focus/cohesiveness and the strongest parts of it are buried in the dreck.

I can get started with a $500 retainer; let me know what you think and we'll go from there. I know time is of the essence for you but I really think you need to put more time and care into the book before you publish it.

Let me know if you have questions or want to discuss...
I'm in and out of the office all week.

Many thanks,
Kelly

[This was an interesting bid. The client had asked me to quote a fee to edit the book, but it needed more than an edit—it needed a complete reorganization. The client agreed and hired me to reorganize the book and then edit (including a lot of rewriting) the manuscript. He was very happy with the finished project, and recently hired me to edit and rewrite the updated second edition!]

Money is Only One Consideration

Finally, remember that while money is certainly important, it's only one aspect of the project you're working on. "My fees have ranged from $5,000 to $40,000. But I often tell people that the price tag is not the only measure of a 'good' ghost gig," says Neuborne. "I've had books that paid $10,000 but were very profitable because the client was smart and had all his material in order. And I've had jobs that paid $30,000+ and were so slow and so disorganized I probably lost money. So when you evaluate a ghost job, don't just look at what the client will pay—look at the whole picture."

That's why the four-part test can be so helpful, especially if you're new to the ghosting field. My first $2,500 book advance paid only a few bills but launched my book-writing career—which later led to my ghostwriting career. If you don't have a ghosting credit under your belt yet, you may want to charge less for your first project to get started.

"It's really important to get your first ghosting project to start ghostwriting," says Turner. "You have to prove you can do it because having done your own book isn't necessarily a qualification to get great ghosting projects…you may have to take less money or do something on spec, but that first ghostwriting gig is your ticket to getting other work."

In a similar vein, you may charge less depending on the state of your bank account. I recently took on a ghosting project for less than I'd usually charge—but I needed the work. My hourly rate wound up being lower than I'd like, but it was still high enough for me to make what I *need*, if not what I want, to make.

No matter what you charge, and how, I suggest you get a retainer up front. First off, it ensures that your client is serious about his project, and it protects you in the event that he decides not to go forward—after you've already written a chapter or done other work for him. A simple letter of commitment that specifies how much and how you'll be paid can serve as your contract until you have a more formal agreement in place, assuming the latter is necessary. [You'll find sample contracts in the next chapter.]

Talking Taxes

Finally, in a chapter about money and what to charge, I'd be remiss if I didn't talk a little bit about business expenses, namely what you can, and cannot, deduct from your gross income.

You probably already know that when you're self-employed, all money you receive from clients (even if it's to reimburse you for expenses) must be reported as income to the Internal Revenue Service. But if you're in the ghostwriting *business*, as opposed to ghostwriting as a hobby, you can deduct legitimate business expenses from that income and only pay taxes on the difference—your net income.

While the IRS takes a number of factors into account to determine whether someone is operating as a businessperson or hobbyist, the primary one is having a "profit motive." In other words, you're pursuing work as a ghostwriter to make money. And as that's the whole point of this book, I'll assume you're doing that.

When you're self-employed, you can deduct all ordinary, necessary, and reasonable expenses that are incurred as you run your business and try to make it a profit from it. For ghostwriters, those expenses typically include:

- Computer (doesn't matter if you're a PC or a Mac!) and other office peripherals like a scanner/copier;
- Office supplies like paper, printer cartridges, business cards, pens, highlighters, and thank-you notes;
- Postage/mailing costs;
- Membership fees to professional and writing-related organizations;
- Office equipment—e.g., desk, office chair, and file cabinets;
- Travel and entertainment related to your business (for example, flying to interview key sources or taking a client out to lunch. However, while you can deduct all of your work-related travel expenses, you can only take 50% of

meals/entertainment costs);

- Internet access, website hosting, and other online fees;
- Telephone expenses (you can't deduct the expense of your primary phone line, but you can deduct long-distance charges related to your business as well as the cost of a second phone line and/or cell phone solely used for business); and
- Car expenses. The majority of self-employed writers use the standard mileage deduction, which in 2013 is $0.565/mile.

In addition, if you're self-employed, you may be able to deduct the cost of medical insurance premiums for yourself, your spouse, and your family. You may also be able to take a home office deduction if you work from home and use a section of it (be it a room or part of a room) *solely and exclusively* as your place of business. (Don't worry—you can still work at your local coffee shop for a change of scenery. I'm a regular at my favorite Caribou. But most of your work should be done from your home office, and you shouldn't be doing anything non-work-related there either.)

I'm not a tax professional (hey, I'm not even a lawyer anymore), so if you have questions, talk to an accountant or visit www.IRS.gov for more info. (*The Tax Guide for Small Business*, Publication 334, is especially helpful.) Track all of your writing-related expenses and keep your receipts so in the rare event you're audited, you have proof of what you spent on your business, when, and why.

Chapter 7

Get It in Writing: Ghosting and Collaborating Contracts

Years ago I was presented with a wonderful opportunity. A well-known sports nutrition expert contacted me about coauthoring a book with her. I'd interviewed her in the past for various articles, and I was excited about launching my coauthoring career.

We talked about her idea, and about writing a book proposal, and agreed to a 50/50 split of the proceeds from a book deal. I agreed to write the proposal—for free. Let me say that again. I agreed to write the proposal for free. We shook hands (she was in Chicago for an event) and I jumped on a train and headed back home to spend eight weeks writing a killer book proposal, including a sample chapter. She approved it and my agent (now working with her on the book) started sending it out. Then we got interest from a publisher—and my coauthor balked. She didn't want to do the book with this particular publisher.

As we had no other offers, my agent and I were hamstrung. The advance was going to be sizable, but without her cooperation, I couldn't proceed. The book died on the vine, and I was left with nothing to show for eight weeks' worth of work...other than having learned an important lesson—actually two.

Lesson number one: that was the one time (and will be the only time) I've written a proposal for a client for nothing. I will not do that again. I don't care how much "best-selling potential" a book idea has, how much promise, how huge the person's platform is. If it doesn't sell, you're out weeks' worth of time with no money to show for it. There's another problem with working for nothing. When you do so, you're devaluing your work to your ghostwriting client. Plenty of people undervalue writers' work—let's not do it ourselves.

Lesson number two: I didn't get anything in writing. Um, I was a lawyer in my former life, remember? Shouldn't I know better? But I'd worked with this person, and we'd shaken hands…I didn't feel it was necessary. That was a much stupider thing to do. (Happily, not all of the work I did on that proposal—which I retained the rights to—was completely for naught. I've since collaborated on and ghostwritten nutrition books…so I did put all that knowledge to good use. But I still would have rather had that fat, juicy book deal.)

Beyond a Handshake

When working as a collaborator or ghostwriter, a written contract is essential. But what elements should your contract provide? What happens if one of you decides you want out of the deal? How can you protect yourself if a client refuses to pay or otherwise breaches the agreement?

The complexity of your written contract will depend on the type of project you're working on, but there are certain elements that should be included in every collaboration agreement, whether you are a ghostwriter or a coauthor. Those elements include: a description of the work, the amount of money you'll be paid, who will own copyright to the work, and the deadline for completing the project. That is the most basic collaboration agreement.

When producing content for big companies, chances are your client will offer you a contract to sign that almost always specifies that you're selling all rights to your work. However, if you have to create your own, a simple contract will suffice. On the following pages you'll find a brief letter of agreement and a template I've used for ongoing ghostwriting work with my comments in brackets:

Hi, Debbie!

Just to confirm that we'll be talking today at 1:00 pm central time for a brief interview re: this article on webcasts; I've already reviewed the material you sent me.

As we agreed, I'll be ghosting an article for you on your venture into webcasts that you'll submit to a professional journal. I'll write a 400-word article for which you'll pay me $400, for $1/word, within two weeks of accepting the article. As we discussed, you will own the copyright to the article, which means you will be free to use it however you wish, once I've been paid for my work.

Please reply to this email and let me know that you agree to these terms. Talk to you later today, and thank you! I'm looking forward to working with you.

All my best,
Kelly

[This email is short, yet includes the necessary terms for an enforceable contract. Note that copyright doesn't transfer to my client until after she pays me for my work.]

Here's a brief sample contract:

Contract

This agreement is made in CITY, COUNTY, Illinois, on _____, 2013, between CLIENT and Kelly James-Enger ("KJE"), a ghostwriter. CLIENT has retained KJE to perform ghostwriting writing, editing, and other related services, and the parties have agreed to the following terms:

1. KJE shall write articles and other pieces for CLIENT on mutually-agreed topics and mutually-agreed deadlines and be a paid a rate of $1/word. KJE will provide client with written invoices on a monthly basis; CLIENT agrees to pay KJE within 14 business days of approving her work.

2. KJE's relationship to CLIENT is that of an independent contractor, not an employee, and KJE shall be responsible for her own social security taxes and other federal and state income taxes. KJE shall bear her own ordinary business expenses including but not limited to telephone and fax charges, postage, copies, and mileage.

3. The parties agree that any and all work KJE performs for CLIENT is a work-for-hire and copyright shall be owned by CLIENT once CLIENT has paid KJE for her work. However, CLIENT agrees to allow KJE to use samples of CLIENT in her online portfolio and for other marketing purposes. Any exceptions to this policy shall be in writing.

4. This agreement can be terminated by either party by giving 30 days' written notice to the other party or by mutual agreement of the parties. If the agreement is terminated, KJE agrees to complete any unfinished work and submit a final invoice to CLIENT within 30 days and CLIENT agrees to pay any balance owed within 14 business days of receiving said invoice.

5. This agreement can be amended at any time by written agreement of the parties.

_____

CLIENT

_____

Kelly James-Enger

[This contract is short but encompasses the basics. Note I've included a clause about copyright transfer; a clause specifying payment within 14 days; and language that gives me permission to show potential clients samples of work I produce for this client. I suggest you include similar provisions—if a client doesn't like them, you can negotiate your contract terms, but why not write a contract that's most beneficial to you?]

Contracts for longer projects, such as book proposal and books, are more complex. As discussed last chapter, you'll want to consider addressing other issues as well, such as:

- The division of labor. Are you interviewing the client and writing chapters for her review, or will she be doing any of the writing? Is the client responsible for providing you with data, research, "war stories," potential sources, or other material, or will you be researching the book in addition to writing it? Will you be conducting interviews with the client or with other people as well? In other words, who is doing what?
- Deadlines. In addition to a project deadline, you may also want to specify deadlines for drafts or sections of the book to help keep you (and your client) on track. If you're working with a book packager or corporate client, you should expect to have a specific timeframe for various elements of

the project.

- Turn-around times. How long does your client have to review material and return it to you for edits?
- Rewrites/edits. If you're charging by the hour, this may not be an issue. But if you're working for a set fee, you'll want to limit your rewrites. For example, Jill Amadio's standard contract includes that she'll do two free rewrites; after that, she charges by the hour for additional changes.
- Method and style of payment. Yes, you're going to be paid, but how much and at what times? Will you have a retainer at the outset, and how much? For example, book packagers often have a payment schedule where writers are paid a percentage of the total fee as they complete sections of the book. Clients will want to distribute your pay over time—I have yet to find one who's willing to pay me my total fee *before* I do any of the work! Bummer.

   Often I will ask for one-third of the amount upfront, another one-third upon completion of the first draft, and one-third upon completion of the final draft. Amadio asks for one-third upfront, one third at the word count halfway mark, and one-third upon approval of the final manuscript. "I also include a clause stating that approval cannot be unreasonably withheld," adds Amadio. "One client held up final payment for months because she wanted to wait until her daughter, serving abroad with the Peace Corps, came home to offer a critique." If the book is to be published commercially, Amadio always shares copyright and asks for a percentage of royalties as well.
- Indemnification provisions. You don't want to be sued over libelous or plagiarized material your client provides, so you may want to consider including language that addresses that. (An indemnification provision, seen in many freelance contracts, puts the burden of any lawsuits or claims on the other party. In this case, as the writer, you should be indemnified for material provided by your client.)
- Cover credit. If you're a ghostwriter, it's safe to assume your name won't be showing up on the cover of the book. *Maybe* your client will mention you in the acknowledgments...or maybe not. If you're coauthoring, you'll want to specify how you and your coauthor's names will appear on the cover, if

it's important to you. Will it be in same-sized type? Whose name will appear first? Will you be described with an "and" or a "with"?

- Copyright. Who will actually own the rights to this book? If it's a ghostwritten book, your client will almost always want to own the copyright. (More about copyright in a bit.) If you coauthor a book, you may hold copyright jointly with the client. Or, the client may retain copyright with the contract spelling out how royalties and other proceeds from the book will be distributed. (For example, with one of my coauthor projects, the client owns the copyright, but our contract with the publisher states that we share all proceeds from the book 50/50, which is fine with me.)

- Termination provisions. What happens if one of you wants to back out before the book or project is complete? What if one of you dies? Consider addressing this "downer" as well—every contract should have an exit clause to protect each of you.

- Expenses, and how they'll be shared. Often expenses aren't an issue. But let's say you're coauthoring a book for a big publisher, and your client decides to hire an expensive publicist. Or what if the book you're ghosting for a client requires travel or transcription services? Who's on the hook for that? Ideally as a ghost or coauthor, all money should be flowing to you; you shouldn't be expected to pay any expenses related to the book other than your usual overhead.

If you have an agent, she should have templates you can use. If not, you need your own templates that you can customize for each client and project. In the pages that follow, you'll find samples of collaboration contracts, consulting agreements, and other documents you'll use as a ghostwriter or coauthor.

The first is a simple consulting agreement I've used when working with clients who prefer to pay by the hour. The second is a collaboration agreement for a ghostwritten book proposal. My client wasn't willing to commit to using me as the ghost for the book itself (see paragraph seven); if she was, I would have included language to that effect:

Consulting Agreement

This agreement is made in CITY, COUNTY, Illinois, on

_____, 2010, between CLIENT and Kelly James-Enger ("KJE"), a self-employed writer and consultant. CLIENT has retained KJE to perform writing, editing, and other related services, and the parties have agreed to the following terms:

1. KJE shall provide writing, editing, and other related services to CLIENT and at a rate of $100.00 per hour; she will invoice CLIENT monthly. KJE shall bear her own ordinary business expenses including but not limited to telephone and fax charges, postage, copies, and mileage; upon agreement of the parties, KJE will be reimbursed for unusual or extraordinary expenses incurred by KJE in her work for CLIENT. Onsite meetings will be charged at KJE's regular rate.

2. KJE's relationship to CLIENT is that of an independent contractor, not an employee, and KJE shall be responsible for her own social security taxes and other federal and state income taxes.

3. KJE agrees to abide by the confidentiality agreement signed on January 21, 2010.

4. This agreement can be terminated by either party by giving 30 days' written notice to the other party or by mutual agreement of the parties. If the agreement is terminated, KJE agrees to complete any unfinished work and submit a final invoice to CLIENT within 30 days and CLIENT agrees to pay any balance owed within 14 business days of receiving said invoice.

5. The parties agree that any and all work KJE performs for CLIENT is a work-for-hire and copyright shall be owned by CLIENT.

6. CLIENT agrees to indemnify KJE and hold her harmless against any claim, demand, suit, action, proceeding, or expense of any kind arising from or based upon language, information, advice, citations, anecdotal matter, resource materials, or other content of the work that was provided by CLIENT.

7. This agreement can be amended at any time by written agreement of the parties.

_____

CLIENT

_____

Kelly James-Enger

Here's a collaboration agreement where I'm coauthoring instead of ghosting:

Coauthoring Collaboration Agreement

THIS AGREEMENT is made on the _____ day of _____, 2010, by and among CLIENT of CITY, STATE (hereinafter referred to as CLIENT) and Kelly James-Enger of Downers Grove, Illinois (hereinafter referred to as James-Enger). The parties agree as follows:

1. Subject to the terms and conditions herein, CLIENT and James-Enger agree to collaborate exclusively with each other in the preparation of a book proposal based on CLIENT's book idea.

2. The fee for the proposal will be $5,000, payable to James-Enger in the following amounts:
$2,000.00 to James-Enger upon signing of the agreement;
$1,500.00 to James-Enger upon delivery of the draft of the proposal;
$1,500.00 to James-Enger upon delivery of the final proposal, including one sample chapter.

3. CLIENT and James-Enger will work together to create the proposal, and determine mutually-agreeable deadlines at the outset for the delivery of the draft and final proposals. James-Enger will provide one revision of the proposal for the stated fee; other changes requested by CLIENT will be billed at a rate of $100/hour.

4. Copyright in the book proposal, in all forms and languages throughout the world, shall be held in the name of CLIENT.

5. CLIENT agrees to indemnify James-Enger and hold her harmless against any claim, demand, suit, action, proceeding, or expense of any kind arising from or based upon language, information, advice, citations, anecdotal matter, resource materials, or other content of the work that was provided by CLIENT.

6. Either party can terminate this agreement by giving the other party written notice; if the agreement is terminated before completion, CLIENT agrees to pay James-Enger for work already performed under the agreement.

7. This agreement sets forth the entire understanding of the parties hereto and may not be changed except by written consent of both parties. If CLIENT acquires a book publishing contract, she can choose to work with James-Enger or with another writer on the book manuscript.

8. The terms and conditions of this agreement shall be binding upon, and the benefits thereof shall inure to, the respective heirs, executors, administrators, successors, and assigns of the parties hereto.

9. Both parties to this agreement warrant that they have no other contractual commitment which will or might conflict with this agreement or interfere with, or otherwise affect, the performance of any obligations hereunder.

10. This agreement shall be construed in accordance with the laws of the State of Illinois.

11. Should any controversy, claim, or dispute arise out of or in connection with this agreement, such controversy, claim, or dispute shall be submitted to arbitration before the American Arbitration Association in accordance with its rules, and judgment confirming the arbitrator's award may

be entered in any court of competent jurisdiction.

IN WITNESS WHEREOF, the parties hereto have set their hands on the date first above specified.

_____

CLIENT

_____

Kelly James-Enger

The preceding agreement is relatively simple. A similar contract will work for a book you're writing for a client who plans to use a print-on-demand ("POD") publisher, or simply wants to pay you a set fee for your work. But what if you're writing a book proposal that will (hopefully) result in a book deal with a traditional publisher? You'll need to address how the advance will be split, as well as royalties.

I call this next agreement my "big dreams" contract because of its escalating royalties clauses. It took us time to hammer out the appropriate percentages, yet the book never sold! You can set any percentage of royalties you want (as long as your client agrees); just make sure it's in writing.

Note that I'm requiring an advance of at least $30,000 to write the book. (I'd already written the book proposal for $15,000 under a separate contract.) And while this contract includes an agent, a similar agreement between coauthor or ghost and client, omitting the agent's involvement, would work too:

Collaboration Agreement

THIS AGREEMENT is made on the _____ day of _____, 2005, by and among CLIENT of STATE (hereinafter referred to as CLIENT); Kelly James-Enger of Downers Grove, Illinois (hereinafter referred to as James-Enger); and LITERARY AGENT (hereinafter referred to as AGENT). The parties agree as follows:

1. This agreement shall become binding on the parties only upon (a) the completion and delivery by CLIENT and James-Enger of a book proposal marketing package (the "Proposal") for a book-length manuscript dealing with the

subject of TK (the "Book") and (b) written acceptance of such package by AGENT as being complete and adequate for purposes of marketing the Book to potential publishers.

2. Subject to the terms and conditions herein, CLIENT and James-Enger agree to collaborate exclusively with each other in the preparation of the Book.

3. It is understood and agreed that James-Enger has prepared the Proposal with CLIENT's assistance and input and has been paid for her work.

4. AGENT shall offer to publishers the opportunity to publish the Book and diligently endeavor to obtain the best possible terms for publication of the Book. No publishing contract for the Book shall be executed by AGENT without the approval of CLIENT and James-Enger, which approval shall not be unreasonably withheld or delayed provided that any such contract shall meet the following minimum standards: (a) a minimum advance of thirty thousand dollars ($30,000), (b) standard book royalties and licensing splits between authors and publisher; and provided, further, that neither of the authors shall have made a substantive objection to the publisher or contract terms. No other type of agreement, other than a book publishing contract, with respect to the disposition of any rights in the Book shall be executed by AGENT without the approval of CLIENT and James-Enger, which approval may be withheld for any reason by either of them.

5. It is understood and agreed that, upon the acceptance of a publishing contract by CLIENT and James-Enger, the actual writing of the Book shall be the responsibility of James-Enger. CLIENT agrees use his best efforts to furnish James-Enger with such materials and information as shall be reasonably necessary for preparation of the manuscript based, on a timely basis, to permit James-Enger to meet such manuscript delivery date as may be reasonably required by the publisher under the publishing contract. James-Enger shall use her best efforts to meet such manuscript delivery

date as may be reasonably required by the publisher under the publishing contract. James-Enger agrees that, prior to the delivery of each draft of the Book to the publisher, she shall deliver such drafts to CLIENT for CLIENT's review, comment and approval, and CLIENT shall promptly review and comment on such drafts in writing. James-Enger agrees to revise the drafts according to CLIENT's reasonable recommendations.

6. CLIENT and James-Enger agree to revise the text of the Book to comply with the publisher's reasonable requests, if any, provided that in no event shall either CLIENT or James-Enger be required to make substantive changes to the ideas express in the Book proposed by the publisher with respect to which either of them disagrees.

7. AGENT shall make best efforts to include in the Publisher's contract that the title of the work in all and any English-language publication throughout the world shall be subject to the prior written approval of CLIENT and James-Enger.

8. The names of both CLIENT and James-Enger shall appear on the work, in all forms and languages throughout the world, separated by the word "and" or the word "with" as the authors may decide between them is appropriate. The name of CLIENT shall precede the name of James-Enger, but both names shall be identical in size and type style.

9. Copyright in the work, in all forms and languages throughout the world, shall be held jointly in the names of CLIENT and James-Enger.

10. CLIENT agrees to indemnify James-Enger and hold her harmless against any claim, demand, suit, action, proceeding, or expense of any kind arising from or based upon language, information, advice, citations, anecdotal matter, resource materials, or other content of the work that was provided by CLIENT. James-Enger agrees to indemnify CLIENT and hold him harmless against any claim, demand,

suit, action, proceeding, or expense of any kind arising from or based upon language, information, advice, citations, anecdotal matter, resource materials, or other content of the work that was provided by James-Enger.

11. Costs of photocopying and other ordinary expenses in connection with preparation of drafts of the Book shall be borne by James-Enger.

12. CLIENT and James-Enger hereby retain AGENT to represent them in connection with the work on an exclusive basis for a period of twelve (12) months after acceptance of the final book proposal package_____ from the date first set forth above, and AGENT shall retain for services rendered fifteen percent (15%) of all monies received under the publishing contract. AGENT's commission for the licensing of individual subsidiary rights, should she license them by approval of CLIENT and James-Enger, shall be in accordance with the commission terms listed in the individual Agency Agreements of CLIENT and James-Enger.

13. Upon receipt of statements from the publisher, AGENT shall promptly dispatch copies to CLIENT and James-Enger. Upon receipt of any monies from the publisher under the publishing contract, AGENT shall promptly disburse such monies, less only the 15% agency commission described in paragraph 12, to CLIENT and James-Enger in the proportions hereinafter specified.

14. CLIENT and James-Enger, jointly or separately, or their authorized representative(s), shall have the right to examine the records of AGENT pertaining to the Book, upon request during normal business hours.

15. All proceeds and revenues received from the sale, lease, license, or other disposition of any rights in the work, throughout the world, shall be divided between CLIENT and James-Enger as follows:
(a) Of the first installment of the advance stipulated in the original publishing contract, James-Enger shall receive

fifty percent (50%), less only agency commission, and CLIENT shall receive fifty percent (50%), less only agency commission.

(b) Of the remainder of the advance stipulated in the original publishing contract, James-Enger shall receive fifty percent (50%), less only agency commission, and CLIENT shall receive fifty percent (50%), less only agency commission.

(c) Thereafter, CLIENT and James-Enger shall each receive fifty percent (50%), less only agency commission, of all royalties received in connection with publication of the Book until the following royalty amounts are reached:

(1) royalties (including advance) in excess of $250,000 but less than $350,000 shall be divided as follows: James-Enger shall receive 45% and CLIENT shall receive 55% of revenues, in each case less agency commission;

(2) royalties (including advance) in excess of $350,000 but less than $450,000 shall be divided as follows: James-Enger shall receive 40% and CLIENT shall receive 60% of revenues, in each case less agency commission; and

(3) royalties in excess of $450,000 (including advance) shall be divided as follows: James-Enger shall receive 35% and CLIENT shall receive 65% of revenues, in each case less agency commission.

16. The term of this agreement shall be co-extensive with the life of the copyright in the Book.

17. This agreement, together with the Book Proposal between CLIENT and James-Enger and any agency agreement entered into by and among CLIENT, James-Enger and AGENT sets forth the entire understanding of the parties hereto and may not be changed except by written consent of all the parties.

18. The terms and conditions of this agreement shall be binding upon, and the benefits thereof shall inure to, the respective heirs, executors, administrators, successors, and assigns of the parties hereto.

19. All parties to this agreement warrant that they

have no other contractual commitment, other than the Book Proposal agreement between CLIENT and AGENT, which will or might conflict with this agreement or interfere with, or otherwise affect, the performance of any obligations hereunder.

20. This agreement shall be construed in accordance with the laws of the State of Illinois.

21. Should any controversy, claim, or dispute arise out of or in connection with this agreement, such controversy, claim, or dispute shall be submitted to arbitration before the American Arbitration Association in accordance with its rules, and judgment confirming the arbitrator's award may be entered in any court of competent jurisdiction.

IN WITNESS WHEREOF, the parties hereto have set their hands on the date first above specified.

_____

CLIENT

_____

COLLABORATOR

_____

LITERARY AGENT

In some cases, your client may ask you to work on an hourly basis and only require a simple consulting agreement. A sample follows.

Dear _____:

This is a brief note to memorialize our conversation this morning, in which we agreed to begin working in good faith on your project, on an hourly basis at the agreed upon rate ($___/hr), as we continue to finalize the language and other terms of our collaboration.

Toward that end, and per your request, I have emailed

a copy of my standard agreement, which includes the terms we have discussed, to your attorney for his review. Also per our conversation, in the event we are unable to come to terms on a formal collaboration agreement, we agreed that I would still be paid for every hour I worked.

Please let me know if this does not reflect your understanding of the above.

All best,
Ed Robertson

I tell clients from the outset that any information they provide me will be confidential. (That's part of the ghostwriting business, even if you don't take a client on.) But sometimes clients want me to sign a confidentiality agreement. No problem—I use an agreement similar to the one below:

Confidentiality Agreement

It is understood and agreed to that the below-identified discloser of information may provide certain information that is and must be kept confidential. To ensure the protection of such information, and to preserve any confidentiality necessary under any applicable laws, it is agreed that:

1. The Confidential Information to be disclosed can be described as and primarily includes information relating to a proprietary book/media idea that is the creation of the discloser.

2. The Recipient agrees not to disclose the confidential information obtained from the discloser to anyone unless required to do so by law.

3. This Agreement states the entire agreement between the parties concerning the disclosure of Confidential Information. Any addition or modification to this Agreement must be made in writing and signed by the parties.

4. If any of the provisions of this Agreement are found to be unenforceable, the remainder shall be enforced as fully as possible and the unenforceable provision(s) shall be deemed modifiable to the limited extent required to permit enforcement of the Agreement as a whole.

WHEREFORE, the parties acknowledge that they read and understand this Agreement and voluntarily accept the duties and obligations set forth herein.

Recipient of Confidential Information:

Name:
Signature:
Date:

Finally, some clients (especially book packagers and corporations/nonprofits) will want you to commit to a schedule for your project. Here's a template you can use as a starting point:

Dear PACKAGER:

Thanks for your time last week. I'm excited about working with CLIENT; you'll recall that I've agreed to ghost this 40,000-word book for $15,000, and I understand it's a work-for-hire.

My plan for tackling the book appears below. After he and I agree on the basic structure (we're close already), I'll provide him with a list of material/info I'll need to start on the book itself. (I will add material myself, too, with his OK, but I'm talking about types of anecdotes, etc. to include. I'll get this material by phone and incorporate it into the manuscript.) Along the way, I'll edit and add material to each of the seven chapters; I think the intro just needs an edit, and the appendix shouldn't change significantly. I'm planning on the following timeline:

Confirm structure/outline: 02.23.07
List of info to Bob: 02.28.07

Introduction:	03.05.07
Chapter 1:	03.15.07
Chapter 2:	03.26.07
Chapter 3:	04.04.07
Chapter 4:	04.16.07
Chapter 5:	04.27.07
Chapter 6:	05.09.07
Chapter 7:	05.22.07
Appendix:	05.31.07

My plan is to give CLIENT the chapters to review and sign off on as I write, so that when I finish the appendix, the book will be completed.

Look good? Let me know if you need any more information so we can get the contract signed and get going.

All best,
Kelly

In some instances, you may need to secure permission to use work from others in your client's book. Here's a simple template to use:

Permission

The undersigned hereby grants [Author], [Publisher], and any persons and entities authorized by the Author or Publisher a non-exclusive license to reproduce [insert description of material—e.g., author, book title, page number, and quote for which permission is requested] in any and all editions in any media throughout the world of the Author's book tentatively entitled [title] scheduled to be published by [Publisher], and in excerpts from the book in any media. This permission is irrevocable, and shall remain in effect as long as either the book or the licensed material remains protected by copyright anywhere in the world. The undersigned warrants and represents that he/she is the owner of the copyright in the licensed material and has the full right, power and authority to grant the license granted by this permission.

LICENSOR:
    Name
    Signature
    Address
    [If Licensor is a company, print name and title of
person signing and full company name.]
        Date of signature: _____, 2010

Copyright: What Ghosts Should Know

We've been talking about the importance of written contracts, so
let's address one more issue relevant to successful ghostwriting and coauthoring—an understanding of copyright law. When you write an article,
book proposal, or book on your own, you automatically own the copyright to it. As the creator of that work, it's yours. But when you ghostwrite
or collaborate, ownership of written work may get murkier. That's why
you specifically address who owns any written material created by you
(or with you) in your contract. Usually if you ghostwrite, the client owns
the copyright; with coauthored material, the client may own it or you may
own it jointly.

And just what is copyright? According to the U.S. Copyright Office,
"copyright" is a form of protection provided by U.S. law to the authors of
"original works of authorship," including literary, dramatic, musical, artis-
tic, and certain other intellectual rights. Copyright means that the author
of the work has the exclusive right to do what he wishes with his work (i.e.
publishing, distributing, slapping it on a T-shirt) and to authorize others
to do the same.

So as the copyright owner, you (and only you) can do whatever you
want with the work you've created—until and unless you sell, transfer, or
assign those rights to someone else (like a publisher—or a ghostwriting
client). That's copyright law in a nutshell.

New writers often think they have to register their work with the
Library of Congress to create copyright. That's not true. Copyright protection is created concurrently with the work—as you get the words down
on the page (what the law refers to as "in fixed form"), it's also automatically copyrighted. But it's got to be "in fixed form." Those awesome ideas
lurking in the recesses of your brain are not in fixed form and so aren't
protected by copyright law.

Of course there is an exception to every rule. With copyright, the exception is when you are an employee, creating work for an employer. Then, the company you work for owns the copyright to anything you create at work under what's called the "work-for-hire" doctrine. In that case, the writing you do at work is automatically owned by your employer, not you. (Some freelance contracts also have work-for-hire provisions; legally speaking, though, a work-for-hire can only exist between an employer and an employee, not a freelancer and a client.)

Copyright Notice

Simple enough. So then what's with the copyright symbol (©)? Why do people stick that on written work? The reason has to do with something called the "innocent infringement" doctrine.

Copyright notice simply lets everyday people (i.e. those who know nothing about publishing law) that this work is someone's property. If there's no copyright notice on a piece of writing and someone copies or uses it for their own purposes (assuming in good faith that it's okay to do so—what the courts call an "innocent infringer"), that person may not be liable for damages. That's why notice is required—to let would-be innocent infringers know that they can't use your work.

The notice required is the copyright symbol ©, followed by the date the work was first published, and the author's name—for example, © 2013, Kelly James-Enger. That's why books have a copyright page—to help protect the work from no-longer-innocent infringers. Just keep in mind that if you're sending work out to anyone in the publishing biz—agents, editors, whoever—you needn't stick a copyright notice on your work. *They* know it's copyrighted—and it looks amateurish.

Why Register Your Work?

There's one last thing about copyright that ghostwriters and collaborators should keep in mind. Yes, your work is automatically protected by copyright simply by writing it. But if you want *effective* protection, you should register it with the Library of Congress. To pursue a copyright infringement case, it's easier and more lucrative if you have registered your work "in a timely fashion" (within three months of publication) with the LOC.

The copyright statute provides that if you prevail, you can get attorneys' fees (which can easily reach tens of thousands of dollars) and statutory damages—in other words, monetary damages set out by law. (Contrast this to having to *prove* your damages in court, which is much more difficult.) If you've registered your copyright, you can introduce that fact at trial to prove you're the legal copyright owner. That's big. Now if you don't register your work within three months after it's published, you may still have a cause of action for infringement, but you're limited to injunctive relief and/or actual damages—that is, the amount of money you have lost because of the violator's actions, which may be impossible to conclusively prove.

So, once your work is published, you have three months to register it. (Registering is retroactive, which means that registering within those three months protects you back to the publication date.) At the time of writing, fees to register with the Copyright Office were:

- $35 to register work online;
- $50 to register work via paper registration; and
- $65 to register a group of articles or other work for periodicals or database updates.

For more information about copyright registration procedures, visit www.copyright.gov. You'll find the forms you need at www.copyright.gov/forms.

The bottom line? Any coauthoring or ghostwriting contract should set out who owns the copyright to the work you're creating. And make sure that your client understands the importance of actually registering his copyright, unless he's working with a traditional publisher that will do it for him. A registered copyright is the best weapon to protect your work.

Chapter 8

Old School or New Paradigm:
Your Clients' Book Publishing Options

As a ghostwriter, you're a writer first. But for longer projects like books and book proposals, you're likely a consultant as well. That means you need to understand today's publishing options—and advise potential clients about them as well. (I'm talking about working with EJs and PPs—if you're hired by an agent, editor, or book packager, you're there to write the book, not provide publishing advice as well.)

We'll talk about electronic books later in this chapter. But let's start with an author's basic print publishing options today:

- Traditional publishing (think Random House and the like);
- Print-on-demand, or POD/subsidy publishers. For simplicity's sake, we'll call POD/subsidy companies where you pay to have your book published "POD". POD firms provide a host of publishing services for clients, including editing, cover and interior design and layout, and even marketing and distribution. The more services you want, the more you pay;
- POD/printing companies. These firms (we'll call them "POD printers"), like Lightning Source, are for publishers (including self-publishers); they print books to order, sell books, and list books with distributors; and
- "True" self-publishing where you do it all—design the book cover, determine the interior and exterior layout, hire a printer, determine the print run, you name it. Because of the work and time involved, this is rarely an option for your typical client.

What's Right for your Client?

Helping your client determine which publishing option is the best fit for him often entails an explanation of what those options are, and the pros and cons of each. Traditional publishing is what most people think of when they plan to publish a book. A publisher likes your book idea, pays you for the right to publish your book, and puts it in print. Yet it's likely that your clients will have little knowledge of how the book publishing process works—namely, that without a sizeable platform, a traditional publisher isn't likely to be interested in them. Clients also have misinformed ideas about the advance they're likely to get, or their book's best-selling potential.

That's why as a ghost or coauthor, you should inform clients about these four publishing truths:

> **Truth 1:** To sell a nonfiction book, you must have a book proposal. A proposal averages 30 to 50 pages and includes sections about the book itself, its competition, the author and his platform, a marketing and promotion plan, chapter summaries, and at least one (often two, with an unknown author) sample chapter. This document is what is used to approach editors (and agents) to sell the book to a traditional publisher.
>
> **Truth 2:** Yet many (actually most) book proposals do not sell. Writing a book proposal, even a stellar one, is no guarantee of a book deal with a traditional publisher.
>
> **Truth 3:** If the book does sell, there's no guarantee of a sizable advance. In fact, advances are shrinking.
>
> **Truth 4:** If the book is published by a traditional publisher, there is no guarantee that it will earn out, or pay royalties.

If your client has a novel to sell, or a memoir, the approach is slightly different. Then you must have a completed manuscript to pitch editors, along with a query letter. But today, the author's platform is still paramount and your client's chances of having his sci-fi novel or memoir of childhood abuse being picked up is…well, slim. Sorry, but that's the way it is.

When your client "gets" how publishing works, he's more likely to understand that you have to charge to write a book proposal—that you can't work on spec, or on speculation, and hope that the book will sell. He may also decide to use a POD publisher for his book, which obviates the need for a proposal.

While there's no advance up front and your client will invest money to publish a book (in addition to paying you as his ghost), there are advantages to using POD:

- There's no "gatekeeper"—in other words, you don't have to sell your book idea to a publisher to get it in print.
- Because you don't have to sell your book to a traditional publisher, you can get your book in print much more quickly. And "time to press" (i.e. the time between turning in your manuscript and the book appearing in print) is much shorter—say, several months compared to at least a year with a traditional publisher.
- Once your book is in print, you make more money per-book than with a traditional publisher. And you start making money with your first book sale. A royalty percentage for a traditionally published book typically ranges from 7% to 15% of the cover price. Depending on the cover price and cost per-book to produce, POD books usually produce a higher royalty percentage for authors.

Helen Gallagher, publishing consultant and author of *Release Your Writing: Book Publishing Your Way*, has worked with a variety of POD publishers for both her own books and her clients'. "With POD, authors have a faster timeline, the book never goes out of print, and the book reaches your audience without years of rejection," says Gallagher. "Why would an author labor over a terrific book and never have it see the light of day?"

Another advantage is that a POD book, once in print, can help your client build his all-important platform. "Self-publishing or POD does not preclude attracting an agent or publisher later," says Gallagher. However, the books that are likely to be picked up by traditional publishers are the ones that have already sold thousands of copies—and most POD books sell far fewer copies than that, in the neighborhood of 100 copies or less.

"If you're doing a family genealogy, or a church cookbook, for example, where you have a limited audience and once you've given or sold the book to those 200 people, that's it, POD/subsidy publishing is a great solution," agrees Fern Reiss, CEO of PublishingGame.com and author of *The Publishing Game* book series. "It's also an incredible timesaver for the busy corporate executive who needs to have a book to show the media, or for the workshop leader who wants a book to sell back-of-the-room at talks, or for a civic group that wants to do a book as a fundraiser, without investing the time-sink that is self-publishing. These are the cases where POD/subsidy is a wise choice."

However, POD has drawbacks if your client wants to sell lots of books. POD books aren't eligible for review by magazines like *Publishers Weekly, Booklist,* and *Library Journal,* which strongly influence library and bookstore buying decisions. The bottom line is that while your client may convince his local bookstore to carry his book, the vast majority of libraries and bookstores won't purchase POD books. "POD/subsidy books (i.e. iUniverse, AuthorSolutions, Infinity, Lulu) cannot be sold to bookstores or libraries," says Reiss. "So if you publish with one of those companies—now they're calling themselves 'self-publishing' companies, or 'assisted self-publishing' companies to further confuse authors—you can sell from your own website, or on Amazon, but you will not be able to sell to normal bookstore/library channels."

Reiss distinguishes between POD/subsidy publishing and POD/printing, such as what's done through LightningSource.com. The latter is for publishers (including self-publishers) and prints books, lists them with distributors, and takes and fills bookstore orders.

Reiss works as a true self-publisher—she does it all including designing book covers and interior pages, determining print runs, and hiring a printing company to publish her books. Self-publishing (which lets you retain complete control over your book) produces the most income for an author per-book, but most of your clients will want the fastest, easiest way to get their books in print. If you're interested in pursuing self-publishing for your own titles or using Lightning Source to print to-order quantities of books, however, check out Reiss's company, www.publishinggame.com.

POD firms are popping up all the time. Some charge per-book while others charge set fees for different "publishing packages" depending on what the author purchases. Some of the most popular include:

- Blurb www.blurb.com
- CreateSpace (formerly BookSurge) www.createspace.com
- Dog Ear Publishing www.dogearpublishing.net
- Infinity Publishing www.infinitypublishing.com
- Llumina Press: www.llumina.com
- Lulu www.lulu.com
- Trafford Publishing www.trafford.com
- Outskirts Press www.outskirtspress.com
- VirtualBookworm Publishing www.virtualbookworm.com
- WingSpan Press www.wingspanpress.com
- Xlibris www2.xlibris.com

When choosing a POD firm, Gallagher recommends looking for a company that offers a low fee for formatting and producing your book, handling online orders and placing your book in all online databases for retail and library sales. Fees start at about $400+ depending on factors like book size, cover design, and how much assistance you need with book design and layout. POD firms also offer editing and proofreading, marketing packages, some distribution, and other services, all for additional fees.

POD authors earn a higher dollar amount per book than a traditional publisher, in the form of a monthly or quarterly royalty. But your author still has to sell those books—and as a POD author, he's not likely to sell as many as he would with a traditional publisher. And that leads to one more important point you should make sure your clients understand: you can write the book but when it comes to selling the book, that's his job.

Recommending a POD publisher to a client is fine—just don't make any promises on its behalf. I like to give clients a list and then let them determine, based on their own wants and needs, which one to choose.

The E-book Option

There's another option your client may consider—e-books. An e-book, or digital book, is the electronic version of a print book. It can be read on a personal computer or an e-reader like an iPad, Kindle, or Nook. Both traditional and POD publishers produce e-versions of print books (the latter, usually for an additional fee), but here I'm referring to a "standalone" e-book, which has no print edition.

You probably already know that the fastest growing segment of the book market is e-books. Since 2011, buyers have purchased more e-books than print books, and given the lower price and increasing popularity of the former, that discrepancy is likely to grow. The ease of digital publishing means that a writer can create an e-book in the morning and have it available on Kindle and other digital platforms by dinnertime. The process is that fast.

However, that very speediness produces the perception that believe that because it's "only" an e-book, it shouldn't cost as much to write. I disagree. Sure, some e-books are short—10,000 words and fewer while others are as lengthy as print ones (think, 50,000 words and up). But even though a shorter book arguably takes less time to create than one ten times longer, an author who can't write still needs to hire a talented ghost to create his book—and pay him a reasonable amount for that work.

"I've done e-books as well as print books, but I don't do a lot of the former," says Melanie Votaw. "People seem to think e-books should cost less—they think they're not going to take as much time." But a book is a book is a book—whether it's printed or in digital form. The work involved to actually write the book is the same, so you should be paid the same regardless of the form your client chooses to publish it in. Your clients should understand that—even if you have to help them with that concept.

If you contract with a client to produce an e-book, clarify who will be responsible for uploading and formatting the manuscript. You can agree to do this for an additional fee; suggest the client do it himself; or he can pay a company like BookBaby.com to do it. Your client will also need a book cover for an e-book; again, he can design that himself or hire a designer or e-book company to create one. (If you happen to have awesome design skills, you may consider creating e-book covers as well. However, most ghosts I know prefer to stick to writing and leave the visual side of things to other pros.)

Staying Traditional

Looking for Mr. (or Ms.) Agent

If your client wants to pursue a traditional publisher, there may be one more issue to address—whether he'll be working with an agent. Once again, people new to the publishing process often need to be brought up to speed on what literary agents do and don't do, and whether pursuing one is worthwhile.

Many book ghostwriters already have their own agents. In some cases, your agent may take on your client too, and represent both of you. If your client has his own agent, or wants to get one, you can work with that agent or have your agent represent you; the latter is more likely to protect your interests. I've dealt with both scenarios, and worked with other clients who didn't need an agent or didn't want to bother to get one.

If your client wants to pursue a traditional publishing house, and has a strong idea and even stronger platform, an agent makes sense. A good agent has the inside track on the publishing world. She's got contacts with editors at different houses and knows their quirks, likes and dislikes. She's familiar with what they've published before and what they're looking for now. She knows what's selling now, and what's not—and what's likely to sell in the future. As a fulltime self-employed writer, I simply don't have the time to keep up on everything happening in the traditional publishing world. That's the agent's job.

Clients should understand that agents work like personal injury attorneys—they only get paid when their clients do. In other words, they have to sell a book to make any money (the industry standard is 15 percent of the advance and any royalties), so they're only going to take on clients they think will make them money.

If you have an agent and you're approach by a client whose book has traditional publisher potential, ask your agent if she's interested in representing the client. Do not make any promises on your agent's behalf—she may not want a client you think is perfect for her. You can give advice to your client, but stay out of the decision-making process when it comes to publishing choices. Your job is to provide objective information and relevant resources (see the agent section in chapter two) and let your client make the decisions. Then you can follow his lead.

Book Proposals: Do You Need One?

Okay, let's cut to the chase, and say your client wants to find a traditional publisher for his book. He's also willing to shell out the money for a book proposal. Nine out of ten nonfiction books are sold on the basis of a book proposal, not a finished manuscript. Even if your client has a finished book, he'll need a proposal to pitch it to publishers.

At its heart, the proposal is a marketing document. Its purpose? To convince a publisher (from the editor to the sales and marketing staff) that this book will sell enough copies for it to make a profit—hopefully a big one.

Every book proposal should include the following elements:

- An overview, which introduces the book's hook, basic concept, and the author's platform;
- A description of the audience (in other words, buyers!) for the book;
- An "about the author" section which is all about platform, platform, platform;
- A marketing and promotion section. Today this is arguably the most important element of the proposal because it showcases how the author's platform will help sell, sell, sell this book.
- A competition analysis, which list books that are the similar, and describes how this book is better than the rest;
- An outline of the book itself, including chapter summaries; and
- At least one sample chapter.

If you're working as a collaborator or coauthor, you'll include information about yourself in the "About the Author" section. For a book that will be ghostwritten, however, the proposal will read as though the client had written it himself—unless he wants you to include an "about the ghostwriter" section. I've include a sample proposal (with permission of one of my ghostwriting clients), minus its cover page and sample chapters. My comments appear in brackets after each section.

Proposal Table of Contents

Endorsements

Patricia Bannan will work to secure endorsements from a variety of well-known experts. Pending review of the final manuscript, she has already secured permission to use the following endorsements or a variation thereof:

"The meals and strategies are healthy and realistic and now, right at my fingertips. I expected nothing short of a fantastic guide to healthy living on the go from Patricia. And here it is: a fun, entertaining and easy to use book based on the latest scientific information. Thank you, Patricia!"—Linda Ciampa, R.N., freelance correspondent and producer for CNN Private Networks

"This book is not a fad. It's a plan you'll want to stick with for the rest of your (busy) life."—Jeanne Goldberg, Ph.D., R.D., professor and director of the Graduate Program in Nutrition Communication, Tufts University

"EATING RIGHT...uncovers the Holy Grail of weight loss on the go: A complete, yet simple plan that will actually work for you—and will keep on working. Patricia has created a very doable regimen that shows you how to achieve a healthy mindset, healthy body and healthy relationship with food, regardless of how much time you have to spend."—Anne M. Russell, editor-in-chief, VIV magazine

"Dietitians know that the strongest predictor of weight loss success is personal motivation. Patricia Bannan's diet advice will help you slim down the healthy way."—Carolyn O'Neil, M.S., R.D., past CNN correspondent, nutrition expert and coauthor of: The Dish on Eating Healthy and Being Fabulous!

"When there's no time to cook, it's nice to know there's a guide that can help. Patricia's meals and strategies are natural, delicious and satisfying."—Jackie Newgent, R.D., C.D.N., culinary nutritionist and author of The All-Natural Diabetes Cookbook: The Whole Food Approach to Great Taste and Healthy Eating and The Big Green Cookbook.

[These endorsements are meant to show the connections she has—and will be used to sell the book. Her connections are part of her platform.]

Overview

Eating right? What a laugh. Who has the time?

Today's women barely have time to breathe, let alone worry about their nutritional intake. Whether traveling for work, shuttling kids to music lessons and soccer practice, or simply attempting to make it to the gym at least once a month, if you're the typical woman in her mid-20s to 50s, you're likely to be eating on the run. You don't have time to cook; you don't have time to bring a healthy lunch from home; you don't even have time to actually read a menu. So it's not surprising that the American Dietetic Association's Nutrition and You: Trends 2008 survey found that more than half of women describe "lack of time" as the primary barrier to eating more healthfully even when they want to.

Women aren't just facing time pressures—they're dealing with ever-increasing levels of stress as well. According to a survey last year, one-third of American women describe themselves as "highly stressed;" another 50 percent say they have average stress levels. Four out of ten eat in an attempt to handle their stress; 35 percent experience fatigue at least several times a week; and more than half experience anxiety, depression, and lack of motivation in a typical week. And recent stats from the National Sleep Foundation reveal that nearly two-thirds of Americans experience trouble sleeping at least a few nights a week.

Yet the majority of women want to eat more healthfully—and lose weight, too. A survey of more than 4,000 women last year found that two-thirds of them were dieting to pare pounds. Many have some idea of how they should eat (consume calcium, eat more fruits and vegetables, cut back on saturated fat) but it's putting that knowledge into practice where women fail.

For example, when a typical woman wants to lose weight, she launches an all-out diet attempt, often based on a "breakthrough" plan she's read about or seen on TV. Problem is, these restrictive diet plans are often difficult to follow in the short-term, let alone the long-term, and carrying her Jenny Craig meal to a dinner out with her clients isn't likely to fly. So, she blows the diet, feels that she failed, and is now more stressed (and more unhappy with her weight) than before.

That's no way to eat—and no way to live.

Eating Right When Time is Tight is the answer for these women. Based on the latest research on health and nutrition, it's packed with doable, practical, "no-time/no-brainer" meals and snacks you can grab on the run based on ten "Master Strategies" for eating on the go.

Eating Right will empower readers to make smart choices, even when they're tired, stressed, or overwhelmed—or all three! As a result, they'll have more energy, a happier mood, and lose weight in the process—without suffering. A basic grasp of the Master Strategies and the 140 meals and mini-strategies that are encompassed by them will give readers the tools they need to eat more healthfully, lose weight, have more energy, improve their overall health, and even handle stress better. They'll learn practical "rush-ipes," simple meals and snacks that require just a few ingredients. In addition, if they're moms, they'll set a better example for their kids—and help them create better eating habits as well.

While there are hundreds of diet tomes on the bookshelves, only a handful address eating on the go—and none are aimed specifically at busy, overloaded women in the mid 20s to 50s age group. Whether working outside the home or wrangling children (or, more likely, both), these women are looking for practical, realistic strategies based on proven research that will make a difference in their daily lives. And Patricia Bannan, M.S., R.D., is uniquely qualified to provide that advice.

A registered dietitian specializing in nutrition and health communications, Bannan develops news segments for television stations, writes articles for magazines, and serves as a consultant and spokesperson to PR agencies and industry groups nationwide. Like many women, she struggled with her weight in her teens and twenties (describing herself as a typical "fat-faced kid" who started dieting in her teens). Through trial, error, and education, she developed her nutritional expertise and learned first-hand how healthy eating on the go is not only possible, but what a difference it can make in weight loss and maintenance, energy level, mood, and performance. Armed with experience, education, and enthusiasm, Bannan is passionate about helping women everywhere do the same.

Bannan has significant media connections. She has appeared as a guest expert on more than thirty news shows, including ABC, CBS, Fox, and NBC's Today show. She served as a contributor to Time Inc.'s Health magazine, has written articles for such leading publications as Self and Shape and currently has a nutrition column on glam.com, reaching almost 1 million unique visitors per month. Her numerous print interviews include The New York Times, People magazine, and the Associated Press. She's worked as a freelance producer and correspondent for CNN's New York Bureau, and "Your Health," CNN's weekend health show. In 2009 alone, she generated more than 15 million media impressions in the U.S. and more than 20 million media impressions worldwide.

Patricia also does direct-to-consumer outreach. Patricia's creative and doable health messages reach 6 million people each day through the in-school and corporate wellness programs of Health-E-tips, Inc. She has also been a media spokesperson for numerous organizations and corporations, including Quaker Oats Company, National Tea Council, and Unilever. While this will be her first book, she's planning additional titles that tie into this theme, including Eating Right When Time is Tight for Men, Eating Right When Time is Tight for Moms-to-Be, Eating Right When Time is Tight for Teens, and Eating Right When Time is Tight for People with Diabetes.

[The overview describes the concept for the book, its audience, why readers will want to buy it, and showcases Patricia's platform.]

Target Audience

There are more than 63 million women in their mid-20s to mid-50s in the United States. The "typical" woman this age works outside the home (nearly 46 million do); has children (more than 80% are moms); and tries to juggle the needs of those around her as well as her own. It's not surprising that her diet often takes a backseat to her busy schedule, but the fact is that two-thirds of women are battling weight problems and trying (and usually failing) to cut calories on any given day. This woman is more than busy—she's overloaded, overstressed, exhausted, and probably crabby, and the last thing she needs (much less has time for) is another "diet." EATING RIGHT will appeal to this woman because its meals and strategies save time and make eating healthfully easier...resulting in more energy, a more positive outlook, better overall health, and a trimmer physique.

[With nonfiction books, you want to quantify your audience. How many potential readers are out there? Note that we've included some knowledge of the potential readership and their wants and needs.]

Competitive Analysis

Admittedly the diet, nutrition, and cookbook shelf is a crowded one. Yet there are only a few books that address healthy eating on the go, and none that are aimed at busy women in the mid-20s to mid-50s age group. The primary competition for EATING RIGHT includes:

- *Are You Ready! Take Charge, Lose Weight, Get in Shape and Change Your Life Forever* by Bob Harper (Broadway, 2008). This book, written by The Biggest Loser trainer Bob Harper, includes 240 pages. While he does give some tips on eating on the run, the book focuses on the emotional causes and aspects of being overweight; the book includes a weight loss plan with rather strict diet recommendations and an exercise program.
- *Eating on the Run: Save Time, Manage Weight and Enjoy Foods that Taste Great,* Third Edition by Evelyn Tribole, MD, RD (Human Kinetics, 2004). This book, first released in 1987, updated in 1992 and updated again in 2004, is the closest competitor to EATING RIGHT. At 216 pages, it does address many of the challenges of eating on the go. While a helpful guide, it's not aimed specifically at busy women, and can be improved upon.
- *Eat This, Not That! Thousands of Simple Food Swaps that can Save you 10, 20, 30 Pounds—or More!* by David Zinczenko with Matt Goulding (Rodale, 2008). At 304 pages, this book created the Eat This, Not That brand with photos showing smarter food "swaps." It's packed with info, but it's unlikely that a busy woman would carry this book around to make side-by-side comparisons—that would require time that she doesn't have! And while the swaps may save fat and/or calories, they're not necessarily healthy choices or ones that will provide adequate fuel throughout the day.
- *Eating Well for Optimum Health: The Essential Guide to Food, Diet, and Nutrition* by Andrew Weil, M.D. (Alfred A. Knopf, 2000). This 293-book provides a comprehensive overview of the connection between nutrition and good health, and includes recipes but provides no specific advice about eating well when you're crunched for time.

- *Eat Out, Eat Right: The Healthier Restaurant Guide* by Hope Warshaw, R.D. (Surrey Books, 2008). This recently updated book includes 284 pages and is an excellent overview of eating more healthfully at restaurants but doesn't address many other topics (eating at home, at work, and in the car, for example) that EATING RIGHT will.
- *The Fast Food Diet: Lose Weight and Feel Great Even if You're Too Busy to Eat Right* by Stephen Sinatra, M.D. and James Punkre (John Wiley & Sons, 2006). This 243-page book includes a six-week diet plan and a restaurant guide that provides a few healthy choices at ten fast food chains. It includes some basic nutrition information but is limited in scope to fast-food eating and its rigid diet is based almost completely on fast-food food options.
- *Food Matters: A Guide to Conscious Eating* by Mark Bittman (Simon & Shuster, 2009). This 326-page book explores the idea of how eating foods in their natural state and limiting or eliminating processed foods can not only improve your health but the planet's as well. It includes recipes but isn't aimed at readers whose goal is to improve their nutrition when time is short.
- *Hands-Off Cooking: Low-Supervision, High-Flavor Meals for Busy People* by Ann Martin Rolke David Zinczenko with Matt Goulding (Wiley, 2007). This 184-book provides dozens of relatively easy recipes but addresses only preparing meals at home, not eating on the go.
- *The Healthy Kitchen: Recipes for a Better Body, Life, and Spirit* by Andrew Weil, M.D., and Rosie Daley (Knopf, 2002). This basic healthy cooking book includes dozens of nutritious recipes, but they're anything but quick and easy. (For example, the "simple" vegetarian quiche recipe requires twenty-one ingredients and at least 90 minutes to prepare.) It's an excellent 325-page cookbook, but doesn't address healthy eating on the go—or healthy eating in a hurry at home.
- *Hungry Girl 200 under 200: 200 Recipes under 200 Calories* by Lisa Lillien (St. Martin's Griffin, 2009). Written by the creator of the "Hungry Girl" brand, this book is a collection of recipes that produce servings of 200 calo-

ries or fewer and doesn't address eating on the run.

- *Naturally Thin: Unleash your Skinnygirl and Free Yourself from a Lifetime of Dieting* by Bethenny Frankel with Eve Adamson (Simon & Shuster, 2009). This 294-page book, written by a minor celebrity with no nutrition background, promises that women will get and stay thin by following her advice. There's little direction about healthy eating when you're busy (the sole focus is weight loss) and her strategy isn't realistic for time-challenged women.

- *The Traveler's Diet: Eating Right and Staying Fit on the Road* by Peter Greenberg, (Villard, 2006). This 366-page book is a diet guide for travelers that covers all aspects of the travel environment. Written by a well-known but overweight travel expert, the book provides tips on eating well at the airport, on a plane, at a hotel, in the car and on a boat but focuses on business travelers, not busy women who are "on the road" every day whether actually "traveling."

[There are hundreds of diet books out there, so we focused on some of the biggest sellers, and showed how Patricia's book will differ from (and be better than!) its competition.]

About the Author

Patricia Bannan, M.S., R.D., (www.PatriciaBannan.com) is a registered dietitian specializing in nutrition and health communications. She develops news segments for television stations, writes articles for magazines, and serves as a consultant and spokesperson to PR agencies and industry groups nationwide.

Bannan has appeared as a guest expert on more than thirty news shows, including ABC, CBS, Fox, and NBC's Today show. She served as a contributor to Time Inc.'s Health magazine, has written articles for such leading publications as Self and Shape, and currently has a nutrition column on glam.com, reaching almost 1 million unique visitors per month. Her numerous print interviews include The New York Times, People magazine, and the Associated Press. She worked as a freelance producer and correspondent for CNN's New York Bureau, where she developed daily news stories and assisted on "Your Health," CNN's weekend health show. In 2009 alone, she generated more than 15 million media impressions in the U.S. and more than 20 million media impressions worldwide.

An admitted "fat-faced kid" who started dieting in her teens, Bannan's personal experience spurred her decision to study nutrition and help others eat more healthfully and it remains her passion. She graduated cum laude from the University of Delaware with a Bachelor of Science in nutrition and dietetics and completed her dietetic training at the National Institutes of Health in Bethesda, Maryland. Bannan received a Masters of Science in nutrition communication from the Friedman School of Nutrition Science and Policy at Tufts University in Boston, Massachusetts.

Bannan serves on the advisory boards of the Center for Nutrition Communication at Tufts University and the Schools of Talent and Modeling at Barbizon International, Inc. Her memberships include the American Dietetic Association, California Dietetic Association, American Federation of Television and Radio Artists, and the Screen Actors Guild. She lives in Los Angeles, but travels frequently for work and embraces her "Eating Right when Time is Tight" strategies every day. She will be working with ghostwriter Kelly James-

Enger on this book.

Kelly James-Enger (Ghostwriter)

In 1997, Kelly James-Enger "escaped from the law" to launch a successful freelance career. Since then, the former attorney's work has appeared in more than 55 national magazines including Redbook, Health, Continental, Woman's Day, Family Circle, and Self. In addition to publishing eight books under her own name, she's collaborated on and ghostwritten others including registered dietitian/television host (and best-selling author) Ellie Krieger's first book, Small Changes, Big Results: A 12-Week Action Plan to a Better Life (Clarkson Potter, 2005). In the last five years, she has worked with traditional publishers, book packagers, and private clients on projects ranging from business memoirs to nutrition guides.

James-Enger specializes in health, fitness, nutrition, and wellness topics. An ACE-certified personal trainer, she speaks to audiences throughout the country about subjects including health, stress management, and goal-setting. She's a member of the American Society of Journalists and Authors, and resides outside Chicago with her husband and son. www.becomebodywise.com.

[My bio is included because we wanted to let publishers know that Patricia already has a ghostwriter on board. In some cases your client may not want to mention you in the proposal—I'd argue that you should be included as that lets the publisher know that the tone of the book will match that of the proposal, as you're the one writing both.]

Publicity, Promotion, and Marketing

Patricia Bannan has significant media connections. In addition to serving as a guest expert on more than thirty news shows, including ABC, CBS, Fox, and NBC's Today show, she's a contributor to Time Inc.'s Health magazine, has written articles for such leading publications as Self and Shape and currently has a nutrition column on glam.com which reaches almost 1 million unique visitors per month. In 2009 alone, she generated more than 15 million media impressions in the U.S. and more than 20 million media impressions worldwide.

Patricia also does direct-to-consumer outreach. Passionate about helping adults and children implement simple strategies to improve their lives, Patricia's creative and doable health messages reach 6 million people each day through the in-school and corporate wellness programs of Health-E-tips, Inc. Bannan will use her extensive media connections to promote EATING RIGHT, and is planning a comprehensive, long-term marketing campaign to position the book as "the" go-to title for busy women.

Media Tour Possibilities/Media Placement Plans

In addition to serving as an on-air expert, Bannan has extensive "behind the scenes" experience. She has worked as a public relations and media specialist in the area of food and nutrition for more than a decade. She has been hired by top public relations agencies to book media tours using her own list of contacts at more than 600 national and local television stations including:

- A media tour featuring the lead researchers of a study on lowering blood pressure with low-fat dairy foods that led to national morning show coverage.
- A "Winning Holiday Recipes" satellite media tour featuring Olympic champion and gourmet cook, Natalie Coughlin.
- A "Nutrition for Soon-to-be Moms" satellite media tour featuring Kathy Ireland.

- A "Racing Wives Cook Off" satellite media tour and local press event featuring five NASCAR wives.

Bannan will work with Beth Shepard Communications (www.electricpressrelease.com), a food and nutrition-focused public relations and spokesperson agency, to secure a minimum of 100 media placements in the first year following publication of the book. Press releases and collateral materials to promote the book will be sent out on electricPressRelease.com and PR Newswire. Bannan will secure an industry-sponsored media event to launch the book in New York City or Los Angeles, as well as at least one industry-sponsored media campaign (e.g., satellite or ground media tour) that uses her as a spokesperson. She will also launch and maintain a website and blog to continue to build her platform and readership.

Spokesperson/PR Opportunities

Bannan has worked as a spokesperson for companies and associations including:

- California Raisins. Services included on-set interviews with news stations in top media markets.
- California Tomato Commission. Services included serving as the expert on a one-hour national radio show.
- Hormel/ Hormel National Choice 100% natural meats. Services included partnering on Shop Smart brochure; an audio news release; being quoted in press release and mat release; print interviews; writing bi-lined articles for parenting publications; TV interviews in major media markets.
- Lean Cuisine. Services included serving as expert spokesperson at numerous community health events in New York City.
- Naked Juice/ Naked Juice Probiotic. Services included on-set interviews with news stations in top media markets about the health benefits of probiotics.
- National Beer Wholesalers Association. Services

included serving as the expert in a satellite media tour on healthful cooking with beer for the 4th of July.

- National Chicken Council. Services included being quoted in press releases; speaking at national health conventions; and interviews with media.
- Paramount Farms, Inc./ PistachioHealth.com. Services included on-set and print interviews in top media markets about the health benefits of California-grown pistachios.
- Quaker Oats Company. Services included on-set interviews with news stations in top media markets.
- Quiznos. Services included three-days of desk-side briefings with magazine editors in New York City and quotes in press releases discussing their new low-carb flat bread sandwiches and low-carb options at fast food restaurants.
- Snapple Beverage Corporation/ Snapple-a-Day meal replacement. Services included speaking at the launch event in New York City; two days of desk-side briefings with magazine editors in New York City; a video news release; a radio media tour; quotes on website and in press releases; and ongoing interviews with media, including The New York Times.
- Tea Council of the USA. Services included on-set interviews with news stations in southern California.
- Tropicana. Services included on-set interviews with news stations in top media markets.
- USA Rice Federation. Services included on-set interviews with news stations in top media markets.

Bannan also works as a communications consultant for top PR agencies representing Fortune 500 companies. She will approach these agencies about possible media tours, spokesperson work, and other promotion opportunities with their clients. These agencies include:

- Burson-Marsteller (www.burson-marsteller.com)

- Edelman Worldwide (www.edelman.com)
- Ketchum Worldwide (www.ketchum.com)
- Middleberg Euro RSCG (www. middlebergcommunications.com)
- Ogilvy Public Relations Worldwide (www.ogilvy.com)
- Pollock Communications (www.pollock-pr.com)
- Porter Novelli (www.porternovelli.com)
- Weber Shandwick (www.webershandwick.com)

Print Media Tie-Ins

In addition, she maintains relationships with writers and editors of many leading publications. She will pitch timely story ideas that promote the book to these and other publications with a minimum goal of ten articles in the first year after the book comes out:

- *Cosmopolitan*
- *Fitness*
- *Health*
- *Men's Health*
- *Prevention*
- *Redbook*
- *Self*
- *Tufts Health & Nutrition Letter*
- *VIV Magazine*
- *Washington Post*
- *Woman's Day*
- *Women's Health*
- *Woman's World*

[Every client should have such a strong platform! Note too that she's committing to actively marketing and promoting the book—she knows what's expected of her and has already developed a marketing plan.]

The Book

Table of Contents

Book Contents/Chapter Summaries

EATING RIGHT will consist of 9 chapters of 20-30 pages each for an approximate length of 250 pages; the manuscript will be completed within 9 to 12 months of signing a book contract. While the book includes "rush-ipes" (simple recipes with minimal ingredients), no photos or illustrations are planned by the author.

Chapter 1
Eating Right – Who Has Time?

You'd eat healthier...if only you had the time. A quick glance at your Blackberry tells you that will happen between today...and...exactly never. And you're not alone. Today's women may have the same 24 hours in a day their moms did, but their to-do lists are much longer—and always growing. Women are overbooked, overloaded, and overwhelmed, so it's no surprise that eating well is a low priority. The irony? The majority of women are overweight, and more than half are trying to pare pounds on any given day. But who can stick to a diet when you're preparing a proposal for your boss, traveling for work, shuttling school-aged kids all over town, swinging by the grocery store, and trying to figure out what to make for dinner...all in the same afternoon? If this sounds like you, take heart—I'm here to help. You can eat better, no matter how busy you are. Better yet, you'll lose weight in the process—without suffering. My simple strategies and solutions will help you do that. And not only will they not take any extra time, they'll often save you time—and boost your energy, improve your mood, and improve your short-term and long-term health.

Chapter 2
Take Ten: The Master Strategies of Eating Right when Time Is Tight

Forget rigid diet plans. To eat right when time is tight, you need a handful of proven, simple strategies that will improve your nutrient intake, your energy, and your stress level. That's where my Master Strategies come in; this chapter will list them and explain the science and reasoning behind them, providing a preview of the remaining strategies in the book.

My ten Master Strategies include:

- Combine protein and fiber.
- Safeguard your environment.
- Munch every morn.
- Eat aware.
- Veg out and fruit up.
- Hit speed bumps.
- Hydrate.
- Energize in 3-5.
- Sweat 30+.
- Recharge.

Chapter 3
Morning Munchies: The Breakfast Boost

You know you should eat breakfast, but who has time? Besides, you're not hungry in the morning, and would rather settle for a late-morning snack or save those calories for later in the day, when you're really hungry. That's bad news for your mood, your metabolism, your energy level, and your overall nutrient intake. You don't have to be a breakfast eater per se, but eating in the morning will make a difference in your performance at work, boost your mood, and cause weight loss-without making any other changes to your diet. Yes, effortless weight loss. Has that got your attention? This chapter will demonstrate why a morning meal is essential, explain why they physiologically crave carbs (cinnamon rolls...yum!) first thing in the morning, and give more than a dozen suggestions for easy, healthy morning meals whether at home, at work, or on the road.

Chapter 4
Noontime Noshing: Eat-on-the-Run Lunch Options

According to a recent study, Americans eat more than 200 meals at restaurants every year—and lunch is the meal most likely to be eaten away from home. Sure you can brown-bag it, but a healthy, quick lunch on the run doesn't have to come from home. This chapter will include several dozen strategies for eating well on the road and at your desk, including the best choices to make at a variety of different types of restaurants (fast food, sit-down, Mexican, Chinese, etc.) Readers will learn how to quickly scan a menu and make a healthy choice, and how to combine convenience store foods or vending machine "treats" for a satisfying, nutritious mini-meal. If desired, this chapter will include photos so readers can "eyeball" appropriate-sized meals and snacks, and learn more about their calorie, fat, and fiber content.

Chapter 5
The Dining Danger Zone:
Supper Strategies that Work

If you're trying to drop a few pounds—and who isn't—dinner represents your most pitfall-laden danger zone. This is where most people "blow it." If you're famished, overwhelmed, or stressed, your motivation to eat healthy is all but gone, which is why on-the-go strategies are so important. In this chapter, readers will learn how to safeguard their environments, use "speed bumps," and what choices make for satisfying yet healthy nighttime meals. This chapter will also discuss why choosing a "lock-up" time for the kitchen (or mini-bar, if you're on the road) is so important.

Chapter 6
Supercharged Snacks:
Eat More Frequently, Lose Weight

People think of snacks as bad, and it's true that a bag of chips or a chocolate bar make a poor choice. However, thinking of snacks not as junk but as mini-meals will improve your nutrient intake, help you maintain your energy level, and aid in weight loss. This is where "energize in 3-5" comes in. Regular snacking is one of the easiest ways to "veg out and fruit up" and increase your overall fruit and vegetable intake, which is key to weight loss. This chapter will also discuss the difference between psychological and physical hunger, and explain which snacks pack the most nutrient punch and have the most staying power.

Chapter 7
Travel Bites:
Eating Well on the Road, in the Sky, and at the Hotel

The average person spends more than three hours behind the wheel of her car every day, adding up to more than twenty hours each week. Frequent travelers rack up even more time in their cars and in the skies. Even with the best of intentions, travel can throw a wrench into your healthy eating plan. Delayed flights, hotel mini-bars, all-you-can-eat buffets, and jet lag can all conspire to sap your energy and your motivation, so this chapter will describe how readers can eat healthy on the road even with few options available, whether traveling for work or pleasure.

Chapter 8
Families, Fetes, and Festivities:
Strategies for Special Occasions

The holidays, wedding receptions, and parties all have something in common—you're likely to overindulge food-wise. The holidays are the hardest time of the year—there's more food around that is higher in calories, higher in fat, and you're likely to be stressed out, sleep-deprived, and struggling to meet your work and family obligations. Safeguarding your environment at home (e.g., "buy fruitcake if you hate it—not your favorite cheesecake"), using speed bumps, "sweating 30+" and opting for healthy but satisfying choices at celebrations will help keep you eating well without feeling deprived.

Chapter 9
Tune in, Tune Out:
Finding some Slow in your Life on the Go

It may sound surprising, but healthy eating on the go isn't just about eating. It's also about taking time to slow down, to de-stress when you can, and to manage your own (likely unrealistic) expectations. Just five minutes of daily relaxation like breathing or meditation can result in huge energy boosts to save you time (and prevent chronic ailments) over the course of your life. Readers will be given a host of stress management strategies ranging from breathing exercises, mind-body exercises like Yoga and Pilates (and more importantly, how to fit them into your day), to why sleep is so critical for health and weight loss—and how to improve the quality of it. This final chapter will build on the nutritional strategies discussed prior and give readers the additional information they need to eat—and live—better when time is an issue.

[I usually write a paragraph for each chapter summary; the sample chapter(s) included with the proposal demonstrates the book's style and voice.]

In addition to the proposal itself, your client may want you to draft a query letter to interest agents or editors. You can charge a set fee for this (that's what I suggest) or include it in the price you charge for the proposal. Here's a template, shared with permission of my client:

Dear TK:

My friend and colleague, TK, suggested that I get in touch with you. I know you represent nutrition and diet books, and have a timely, clever book idea that I hope you'll be interested in representing:

While most of us work to earn a living, there are more than 10 million Americans in demanding careers where productivity is a top priority. Doctors, lawyers, traders, managers, consultants, accountants, business owners, you name it—they're working in fields that demand more than a typical 40-hour work week. While they may possess all of the practical skills necessary to survive in their chosen profession, there's a hidden factor that can affect their mood, their energy level, their performance, their salary— even their future. It's their diet.

Yet otherwise smart, savvy business people overlook the impact of the way they eat (or don't eat) has on their day-to-day performance at work. The main problem? The environments they find themselves in. Busy career pros face four primary environments—the office, travel, dining out, and home—that encourage eating too much of the wrong foods and too little of the right ones. Each environment presents a different series of challenges, and addressing them takes knowledge, planning, and practical skills.

Eat your Way up the Ladder: The Busy Professional's Guide to Nutrition on the Run is a complete lifestyle guide for the businessperson on-the-go. It addresses the four major environments we live in (home, work, eating out, and travel) and helps people make smarter food decisions and break bad habits. Readers will learn not only about the challenges they face as career-oriented professionals but also how their colleagues have faced similar ones—and overcome them. The book will explain what environmental factors impede people from making healthier eating choices, and how to circumvent them—without making eating well a second career.

Follow this plan, and yes, readers will lose weight if they need to. But while there's a new crop of diet books every season, almost none address the impact diet has on productivity. Researchers know that a balanced diet not only improves health and reduces your risk of disease—it also improves mood, energy level, mental cognition skills, and your ability to deal with stress. Those skills are integral for success, whatever your chosen career.

About me: I'm and LA-based nutritionist with five years of experience counseling professionals in a variety of fields. I was the exclusive nutritionist for Discovery Health's "National Body Challenge 2008," and my short clips on a variety of nutrition subjects for Discovery Health appear on "On Demand" cable networks throughout the country. I'm frequently quoted in the media, and am continually building and expanding my platform. I'm committed to making this book a success, and have already begun implementing a marketing plan for it.

I hope you'll be interested in reviewing my book proposal for Eat—please let me know if I may send it to you immediately. Thank you very much for your time; I look forward to hearing from you soon.

Very truly yours,
Alyse Levine MS, RD

[This is a strong query letter that opens with an "in," demonstrates the market for the book, and highlights the expert's platform.]

One last thing when we're talking about ghostwriting books. If you're working with a client who wants to pursue a traditional publisher, make it clear that you're being hired to write the proposal, not sell it. (Selling it is the author's job, or that of his or her agent.) I suggest you avoid making any kind of guarantee about the marketability or a book, or how much of an advance a publisher may offer—while you can pen a stellar proposal, you can't make an editor buy it. If you have a client who's serious about getting published and is unable to sell the book to a traditional publisher, you can always suggest that using the outline to ghostwrite the book for a POD publisher instead. In that case, your client will pay you directly to write the book, instead of taking money from the advance to do so. Either way, you still get the gig of ghosting the book.

Chapter 9

From Concept to Cash:
Working as a Ghost

So you've got a ghostwriting assignment. You've convinced your client that you can give him what he wants; negotiated your fee; and signed a contract. What comes next? Actually ghosting the piece.

Ghostwriting isn't that different from writing a piece for a corporate or business client. If I'm hired to write a brochure for a business, for example, I'll ask a series of questions about the company; its customers; the purpose for the brochure; the company's products and/or services; and the features and benefits of those products and services. I'll ask what sets them apart from their competition, and what the client hopes to achieve with this brochure. With that information in hand, I'm ready to write.

When you ghostwrite, you take a similar approach. You need to know not only about the subject you're writing about, but the goal of the piece as well. That extra element is essential to successfully ghost.

After I get a short ghostwriting assignment (e.g., an article or blog post), I typically take the following steps:

- Interview the client (or other source) for background information.
- Conduct additional background research about the topic, market, and/or audience for the piece as necessary.
- Write the initial draft.
- Submit that draft to my client and request feedback.
- After receiving feedback (whether through a phone conversation, email, or edits to the article itself), rewrite the piece.
- Send the revision back to my client, asking for feedback.
- Make any other additional changes, and ask client to sign

off on the piece.

- Submit an invoice, if necessary.
- Get paid!

I always find real-life examples instructive, so here's how I handled a short ghostwriting assignment from a client who was new to me. She found me through my website, and emailed to ask if I'd be interested in ghostwriting a short article for her. We set up a time to talk by phone, and during that conversation I asked the following questions:

- What's the subject of the article?
- Do you have background material I can review to write the article, or will I interview you to get what I need?
- Do you have a market in mind for the article?
- Who is the audience for the article?
- What do you hope to achieve with the article? Do you have more than one goal for it?
- How long does it need to be?
- What's your deadline for the article?

My client wanted an article about her company's new series of webinars aimed at court reporters. We talked a little bit about the article idea and the webinars themselves, and why court reporters might be interested in them. As we were talking, I was taking notes about the way she spoke, and noting key phrases that I might incorporate into the piece; that's key to capturing voice.

After learning that she had a market already in mind—a trade magazine that had agreed to take a look at her piece "on spec," meaning that the editor would consider publishing the piece—and that the piece would be about 400 words, I told her I would charge $1/word for the assignment. Another ghost may have asked for more, but the topic wasn't complicated, and I was confident I could write the article fairly quickly.

The client agreed to my rate, and we set a deadline several weeks away for the final draft. As she was a new client, I expected that my first draft would need some tweaking, and explained that I welcomed her suggestions. I sent her an email confirming our conversation. Two days later, I was online, reviewing her website to learn more about the online classes for court reporters, and wrote the initial draft of the piece.

I sent her the story, and noted that I thought we should interview a court reporter who had taken at least one of the classes. I felt an anecdote from a court reporter would add credibility to the article, and make the piece look less like a PR-generated press release. However, my client wanted to the be the only source for the article, so that's how I wrote the piece.

I emailed the finished piece to her and asked for her feedback. She returned the story back to me with some new material, which I edited and returned it to her. A day later, she made a few more changes and sent those to me; after I incorporated those changes and returned the story to her, she signed off on it.

The total time on the assignment (including the initial phone call with her) was about 4 hours, so I made the $100/hour rate I try to average as a freelancer. She paid me within a week.

Here's the final version of the story. Note that I've double-spaced the manuscript; this is the format I use to turn in articles and books.

Kelly James-Enger   402 words
5736 Webster Street   All rights
Downers Grove, Il 60516
630.795.1288
Kelly@becomebodywise.com

Become a Better Court Reporter From Home:
Webinars Offer New Way to Learn Skills and CEUs

by

[Client Name]

As a court reporter, your career development is in your hands. It's your responsibility to improve your skills and learn new ones as technology changes. That's one reason most states require court reporters to obtain continuing education units, or CEUs.

Even if you live in a state without a CEU requirement,

investing in your career pays off in both the short- and long-term. Now there's an option that makes building a successful court reporting career easier than ever—taking webinars, or educational webcasts, offered through Bridges Court Reporting.

"I was a court reporter before I was a business owner, so I understand the importance of continuing to educate yourself," says Debbie Bridges, owner of Bridge Court Reporting. Bridges decided to start offering webinars to help her company's reporters develop their own skills but quickly realized that other court reporters would benefit from them as well.

"As court reporters, we don't work in a corporate world where our employer trains us. We're isolated. Even if you work for an agency, you take our equipment to the job, and then you go home to edit the job," says Bridges. "You don't have a lot of interaction or discussion with your peers."

Yet traveling for continuing education can present problems. "Court reporters may not want to lose income by traveling or to have to worry about their families," says Bridges. "But now you don't have to travel or wait for once a year—you can learn from the comfort of your own computer." Better yet, studies show that students who learn online retain information better than when they learn in a typical classroom environment.

Current webinar offerings include:

- *Communicating with Emotional Intelligence*
- *How to Become a Repeat Reporter*
- *Is your Dictionary Getting in the way of Realtime?*

When you purchase a webinar, you have unlimited access to it for 90 days. The National Court Reporter Association has prequalified the content of the webinars, and offers 0.10 in CEUs per class. Each webinar costs $37 (or $99 for all three); you pay an additional $40 when you submit a CEU form to the NCRA.

Bridges plans to continue to expand the Webinars to address more subjects including technological and career topics as well as work-life issues. "I'm excited about the lineup because it's material that's needed, and that court reporters can put to use right away," she says. "Our goal is to help shorten the learning curve for reporters, and help them be more successful in their careers."

For more information, visit www.bridgescourtreporting.com/training.php.

-30-

End of story, right? Not quite. My client's chosen market decided not to run the piece. My client was disappointed, but I had explained in our initial conversation that as a ghost, I can write an article but I cannot guarantee that a market will publish it. (This isn't any different than writing a bylined article. I've written stories and turned them in only to see them languish for months—in a couple of cases, years—before they were published. In other cases, I've had stories killed or markets go out of business before an article was published. That is outside of my control.) Because she had the piece in hand, however, she decided to use the article on her website to help promote the webinars.

The length, subject matter (and your familiarity with it), and type of piece you're hired to write will all impact how much time a ghostwriting assignment will take you. I always expect to write three drafts for a new client—the initial draft; the second draft where I incorporate any requested changes or new information; and the third (and hopefully final) draft, which should be accepted by the client. Plan on a similar process when negotiating your deadlines, and confirm how much time your client has to review your work so you can make that deadline.

Of course you don't have to follow my model of working; your approach may differ depending on the client and project. "In my experience, the client has a set agenda already determined for the blog. It is my job to guide the content in a way that makes sense and will be most helpful to the reader," says Jill Russell Qualizza, a frequent ghost-blogger. "At that same time, I need to help my client gain his own new clients and help expand his business while elevating himself as the "go-to" expert in X field. After reviewing a list of topics, I schedule a very basic editorial calendar. This can simply be a list of topics or a more detailed schedule with dates.

"My client works two ways: He drafts an article on a topic. I then review it and we hold an 'interview' where we discuss the topic, and I ask questions that I think we need to answer in the article, or include," continues Qualizza. "I then edit and rewrite the piece. A final round of approvals is made before the article is posted on the blog. Other times, I 'interview' him by guiding him through a conversation (letting him talk and asking questions when I know an audience will want more about a topic) and then go and write an original piece. He'll review once before I make final edits for posting."

Other clients may want to take more control over a piece and give you notes or templates to work with. Qualizza offers these tips for ghosting shorter pieces for clients:

- **Do** treat the piece as a legit, third-party article.

- **Don't** forget you are writing this for your client, and at the end of the day you want to make (and keep) them happy.
- **Do** research the company you are writing for. Find out its goals and learn its product as you would writing about anything else.
- **Do** find the best experts—the client wants their article to be credible, readable and interesting. His credibility is on the line here, just as yours is when you submit an article with your name on it. Just because you've said goodbye to the byline, doesn't mean you say goodbye to your ethics.
- **Don't** solely focus on your client's product or bash the competition. The fine line here is treating this as if it's a "real" article, something a newspaper or magazine would accept and not only in the editorial section.
- **Do** include a call to action. Remember your client's goals and work to cause some action by the end of the article.
- **Do** remember you are writing for someone else...in his voice. Work to find that and incorporate it in your writing.
- **Do** guide the client on important issues, or focusing more on one thought versus another.
- **Don't** let the client landslide your direction and counseling. They hired you for a reason—because you are the writing expert. Be that expert.
- **Don't** be so set in your ways that you don't give the client what he wants. At the end of the day this work reflects on him, so he needs to be happy.

Possibly the most challenging part of ghosting articles, blog posts, and content marketing pieces is capturing the unique voice of your client. As I mentioned, I take careful notes whenever I speak with a client to help determine his speech patterns, word choices, and cadence. I also ask for samples of any material he's written or other examples of what he wants the article to sound like.

It's not that different from writing an article as a freelancer, where you try to match the voice of the publication you're working for. However, as a ghost you don't have a market to emulate—you have to emulate the voice of the client. The key to doing so is listening.

"Listening is the most critical skill a ghostwriter can develop," says Kendra Bonnett, who's the coauthor of *Writing Alchemy: How to Write Fast and Deep.* "I mean, writers are a dime a dozen. But it takes both skill and discipline to listen to others and capture their thoughts and voices and bring those to paper." Bonnett got started early on as a ghostwriter writing papers for her best friend in college. "That's when I learned that ghostwriters need to capture the thoughts and speech patterns of those for whom they are writing," she says. "That's critical. You can't write in your voice. You must write in the voice of your client."

If you're struggling with voice, get your client talking. Ask questions that will draw longer, more detailed answers. "I ask clients questions and get them to tell me some stories," says Kelly Kautz. "I had a blog for a pest control client and the client had a lot of great stories…he told me some of the kooky and strange things hat happened on the job, why he went into extermination, and how he was really fascinated by bugs as a child…the blog had personality and that's what people are looking for—they want to know the company better and the people behind it."

Some clients may provide you with writing they've already done, but like many ghosts, Kautz prefers to speak with a new client to get a feel for his unique voice. "I find getting people to talk off the cuff and getting them relaxed helps me capture their tone of voice and personality," says Kautz. "If you're just looking at what they've written, you may not get that same flavor."

Ghosting Books and Other Longer Projects

Now that we've talked about shorter pieces, let's move into books. Ghostwriting a book takes more than an ability to understand your client's needs and write in a specific voice. To do it successfully, you have to be more than a writer. You must be a project manager, often an arbiter, and sometimes even a therapist. An understanding of these roles will help you regardless of what types of ghosting work you do.

Let's talk about your project management role first. When you write your own book, you do it all. *You* conceptualize, organize, research, write, rewrite, edit, and proofread, all on your own. If you want to change the structure of the book, or take a different approach, that's your decision. You're halfway through and you decide to add more anecdotes or write an extra chapter or two? No problem (though you may have to run that by your editor.) You're the captain of the ship, the master of your domain. You write your book. It's that simple.

When you ghostwrite or collaborate, however, you're adding someone to the mix—namely your client. And that person is going to be involved to some degree. *How much* participation will depend on the project (and we'll talk about different ways to work in a bit) but almost always your client is the primary source of information for the book—and is the one who has to approve your work.

That's where project management skills come in. Let's say you're hired by a publisher to ghost a book for a big-name author with a specific deadline. Guess what? The person in charge of getting in touch with the author and keeping that person on schedule is you. Your client may not be as motivated as you are to finish a book or even keep the project moving forward, but as a ghostwriter you get paid for the work you actually perform. If your client drags his feet or doesn't respond to requests for necessary info, and you can't continue to write, you're not getting paid. (And if you've set aside time to work on this particular project and your client isn't cooperating, you have a big unpaid hole in your schedule, which hurts your productivity, your bottom line, and probably your mental state as well.)

As a ghostwriter, though, you walk a fine line. You're not really this person's *boss* (after all, you're being paid to write *his* book), yet you need to keep him on schedule. This means you have to be able to take charge— without hurting your working relationship or bruising any fragile egos.

That's why I suggest at the beginning of a project, you have a phone conversation or in-person meeting to provide an overview of how you will work, and emphasize the importance of the client's involvement—whether it's being available for phone interviews, providing research or other necessary material, reading and critiquing chapters, or simply answering quick questions via email. I like to give the client a turnaround time at the outset; for example, he has five business days to return a chapter to me with his critiques and changes.

"I've come to the conclusion that I have to have a talk with my client when we begin about how my business works," says Melanie Votaw. "I tell them I'm going to try to stick to deadlines but they need to do that too. If they're going to pay me at a certain time for something based on work done or a timeline or a parameter, I need to know that that's going to happen— because otherwise I'm twiddling my thumbs."

When the client understands the importance of his involvement and responding in a timely fashion to what you need, he's more likely to cooperate throughout the process. And that's good for you and for the project itself. This conversation also helps build trust between you and the client.

"You have to be as clear with the process as possible, especially if you're telling a nonfiction-type of story or working with a business-type person," says Ed Robertson. "They think in terms of bullet points and PowerPoints. So you have to clearly lay out the scope of the project from A to Z so they have a clear direction of what you intend to do. To me, a book collaboration is like a marriage or any kind of personal relationship—a good one is built on trust. You have to establish their trust in you...and I've found that the ability to articulate and bullet-out the scope of the project as early as you can is key."

I also like to use the agreed-to deadline for the book to work backwards to set deadlines for parts of the project, typically chapters. I then send that to the client so we're on the same page and he knows what to expect. For example, when I worked with a sales coach on a book with a tight deadline, I set the following timeline:

- Introduction: 03.05.07
- Chapter 1:   03.15.07
- Chapter 2:   03.26.07
- Chapter 3:   04.04.07
- Chapter 4:   04.16.07
- Chapter 5:   04.27.07
- Chapter 6:   05.09.07
- Chapter 7:   05.22.07
- Appendix: 05.31.07

This is an aggressive schedule, and as the ghostwriter, I worked backwards as well, aiming to have a draft of each chapter to the client for his approval a week or so before each agreed-to deadline. Get the idea? If there are other elements you'll be writing, such as an introduction, bibliography, or index, make sure you've accounted for them as well. I've found that using this kind of schedule keeps work moving along; if the client needs to renegotiate the timeline, we'll work together to create a new one.

Just as with shorter work, I assume that I'll be writing three drafts—the initial one that I submit to the client; the second draft that incorporates any changes/additions from the client; and the third (and hopefully final) draft that the client signs off on. When setting deadlines, I make sure I'm giving enough time for all three drafts (and the back and forth process) to be completed. And when in doubt, always assume that you'll need more time, not less, to finish any part of a ghostwriting project!

Who Does What?

Speaking of working together, how *will* you be doing that? You need to clarify this with your client as there are a variety of ways to ghostwrite or collaborate. What's right for a particular project will depend on the subject matter, your client's writing ability (and interest in writing any or part of the book), your client's schedule, your client's budget, and the timeframe of the project. Some of the ways you may work as a ghost or coauthor include:

- You research and write the book based on interviews conducted with the client (with follow-up questions as necessary). Other than providing you with thoughts and ideas, the client's involvement is limited to reviewing and approving your work.
- You research and write the manuscript based on an outline and material supplied by the client, or conduct research on your own; again, the client's involvement during the writing process is limited.
- The client has written materials (such as draft chapters) that you use as a starting point to create the book; you elicit additional information from him and/or conduct additional research to complete the book.
- The client writes part of the book, you write part of the book, and then you edit the client's material for consistent voice.
- The client has a completed book but hires you to edit and improve the book. (This may start out as an editing job, but often turns into a kind of ghostwriting where you obtain additional information from your client, do more research, or add material to create a stronger, more compelling book.)

Let me give you some examples of how I've worked in the past. *Small Changes, Big Results* is a nutrition/fitness/wellness book. My coauthor, Ellie Krieger, is a registered dietitian, and wrote the nutrition portions of the book as well as the recipes. I wrote the remainder, including the fitness and wellness sections, and then edited her work and pulled it all together. The result was a seamless book that sounded like she had written the entire thing. (We'll talk about capturing a client's voice in a bit.)

When we updated the book nine years later, we followed the same template. She made additions and changes to the nutrition section and wrote new recipes while I updated the fitness and wellness parts of the book by adding sidebars on topics like high-intensity interval training, popular apps that let you track your workout routines, and the latest trends in group exercise classes.

With another project, my client had about a 14,000-word manuscript already written. I used that as a starting point and "grew" the book, reworking his material and adding much more. I interviewed him every week or two and used my notes from those conversations to write the book; he then reviewed each chapter and made suggestions.

Another book was a memoir that started out as an editing job, but his book needed more than an edit—it needed more details, a stronger narrative structure, and some reorganization. After my initial meeting with my client, I sent him email questions and he returned detailed, thoughtful answers. I then used that information to rewrite the book. (If you can convince your client to write up notes or answer questions via email as opposed to always doing phone interviews, this is a huge time-saver...and spares your fingers all that transcribing, too.)

A recent project was more involved on my end as the client told me what she wanted and I researched and wrote her book on my own. I provided her with a brief chapter outline, and upon approval, wrote each chapter for her review. When she asked for edits, I made them. Her day-to-day involvement was limited to giving me a short description of what she wanted in each chapter and a list of websites and other resources for background material.

Even this quick review reveals the breadth of ghostwriting jobs—that's why it's so important to know upfront (*before* you bid on a job) how you'll be working and what material or research a client will be providing you. The most time-consuming and labor-intensive job is when you're assigned a book and research and write it from scratch, with your client's input (which may be minimal).

While I will take any kind of work if the price is right, my favorite kind of project is when the client has *something* down (even if it's a mess) that I can start with. I like taking rough material and cutting, adding, and improving it until it sparkles. Yet every ghostwriter has different preferences and ways of working. Stephanie Golden prefers to start from scratch instead of "wading through a lot of badly written material" while Melanie Votaw, like me, prefers to have something that she can shape and embellish.

The Writing Process

As a ghost, you may be "stuck" with a format that you can't deviate from. Marcia Layton Turner's typical client already has an outline that the publisher has approved. "Then the client sends me background materials and we have phone conferences where we walk through each chapter in order," she says.

There are other cases where you may need to substantially rework a client's book—or deviate from it entirely. Tim Gower worked with a professional client who had already written a book, but Gower knew that his approach wasn't likely to sell to a publisher. "In that case, I used the book more or less as a reference [to write the proposal]. His ideas about how to organize a book wouldn't work for a consumer audience," says Gower. "I reframed it to make it more consumer-oriented." Gower was on the money—the proposal netted a book deal, and he wrote the resulting book with the expert afterwards.

If your client has no outline or no set idea of how to approach the book, though, you'll need to spend some time brainstorming the format of the book itself. Gwen Moran's first step when working with a client is to draft a detailed outline and project overview, which includes a definition of the primary and secondary audiences. "This acts as our touchstone," says Moran. "When there is any question about the work or the content, we can go back to this outline, which we both agreed was the best structure for the book."

Keep it Simple with TK

Ever heard of TK? I introduce every ghosting client to this valuable tool. When I have a question in the text—say I need more info from the client or want him to confirm that I have described something correctly—I put a TK there.

Here's an example from a memoir I worked on. When my client had reported the events that had happened, he tended to leave out details. Often I'd ask him specific questions so I could enrich the book with more color and depth. Here, he was talking about arriving in Santa Domingo to work for Habitat for Humanity. I returned the draft chapter back to him with TKs requesting more information from him:

> ...Arriving in Santo Domingo, we were greeted by Chris and Steve, the couple that operates the Habitat affiliate in Barahona. [TK/descriptions of Chris and Steve] Several years prior, they had decided to leave promising journalism careers at *The Chicago Tribune* to run the Habitat Affiliate in Barahona. They told us they had both felt called to make a difference with the people here, and I was impressed with their relentless energy and enthusiasm.

> [TK/description of Santa Domingo]There were dozens of armed military personnel patrolling the streets and sidewalks you had to keep your passport with you at all time. [TK/you were nervous, scared, what? What did the armed personnel look like?]

When he emailed me back with notes for my TKs, I used that information to rewrite this section. In general, the more detail you can provide, the more compelling it is for readers. And as with any kind of writing, "show, don't tell" is smart advice. "Telling is a narrative form where the writer simply writes what happened and expects the reader to accept the information at face value," says Bonnett, "But when writers 'show' an event, they take the time to dig for information--both facts and descriptive detail…they paint word pictures that make scenes come alive and, often, use dialogue. In this way, readers are able to reach their own conclusion.

In other instances, I use a TK to ask the client for more information or to confirm something I'm unsure of:

> …Later in this chapter, you'll find a list of quick, easy breakfasts on-the-run—and ways to make the best out of less-than-healthy choices as well. [TK/do you want to give me some stuff here on breakfast and hormones…you'd mentioned it before]

I use TK as a reminder for myself as well; then when I go through a draft, I can double-check facts or fill in missing information. For example, here's a line from a book I ghostwrote:

> When it comes to sleep, men have the proverbial leg up. Studies prove that women are more likely to suffer from poor sleep than men. TK

I've written about sleep before, and knew that this was the case. The TK is *my* reminder to find a source or recent statistic to back up my claim and incorporate that into the manuscript.

Get the idea? Using TK is a quick, easy way to request additional info from a client, or draw his attention to a section of your work that needs closer review. I suggest you use it with your clients of both shorter and longer work.

Staying in Touch

Another question to consider is how you'll contact each other. With most of my ghosting work, I never meet the client in person. We talk by phone, and then work primarily by email, sending chapters back and forth. I'll send the draft of a chapter to my client and ask him to review it and make any changes or additions by a certain date; I then review those changes and return it to him for his sign-off. In the past, I've used the

"Track Changes" function in Word, and asked that my client leaves it "on" so I can quickly spot edits he makes without having to read through the entire chapter again.

However, I've since abandoned track changes in favor of highlighting any changes I make in yellow (which is eye-grabbing) and simply making any notes to the client in the manuscript itself with a TK as I mentioned above. I find it easier to review the draft this way. When you highlight any changes in yellow and your client does the same, you'll be able to quickly scan through a second or third draft to review any changes, which saves you (and your client) valuable time.

I try to limit phone calls, preferring to work via email. If the client wants to talk by phone, I ask him to email me and we set up a phone appointment. Why? First, I don't work an 8:00-to-5:00 day. Truth be told, I run a fulltime business in part-time hours...but I'm not going to advertise that to my clients. Second, every phone call is an interruption to whatever I'm working on. And finally, I will make myself available to my client, but I don't want him to think he can call me every time he has a book-related thought he wants to share. That's what email is for.

Of course *when* you work will be somewhat dependent on your client, points out Gower. "You can't entirely make your own schedule when you're collaborating, especially when you're talking about high-powered types," says Gower. "It can mean working a lot of nights and weekends, so flexibility is a really nice quality to have when you collaborate."

Let me give you one more tip about working with a ghostwriting client—touch base with him every so often, even if you don't need anything at the time. You may have other projects in the works, but his book is the only one that's important to him. A quick email every week or so keeping him in the loop takes just a few minutes and makes him feel part of the process—which he is, of course. (Think something like, "Hi, Dick, hope you're doing well. Just wanted to let you know chapter three looks great—thanks for sending your changes—and I'll have chapter four to you by Thursday. Thanks and talk to you soon!")

Writer as Researcher

With some books, your research may be limited to creative questioning of your client. With others, however, you may have to act as a journalist to obtain necessary information and data. If you're written a book of your own or have freelance experience, this shouldn't be a stretch. I still suggest, however, that you get as much material from your client as you can, even if it's just a list of possible resources he wants you to draw from.

The less time you spend researching, the more time you'll have to write the book and the more efficient you'll be.

Your client shouldn't expect to spoon-feed you though. Yes, you're a ghostwriter but you're a journalist as well. Don't be afraid to run with an idea and present it to your client. Let me give you a few examples:

- For a book proposal on a health-related topic, I suggested including a section on stress and how it impacts health. I do a lot of speaking and writing about stress management, so I knew there were interesting studies on how chronic stress can cause a variety of health problems. The client liked the idea, and we included that in the proposal.
- For a book proposal for a different client, I suggested we cite some recent studies and statistics in the overview to help quantify the potential audience for the book.
- While ghostwriting a book, I brainstormed a creative, clever way to approach some of the "how-to" strategies the author wanted to include—and ran it by her. She liked the concept and it worked well with her overall approach.

Get the idea? You may be writing your client's book, but you can always bring more to it than your client expects. Your creativity and your research skills are part of the overall package that you offer to a client. As you write a book, you'll find that you have ideas on how to improve and enhance it. That's part of what makes writing so exciting, even when you're creating someone else's book.

Capturing your Client's Voice

We talked a little bit about voice earlier in this chapter, but writing in a client's voice for an entire book can be more challenging. Pay attention to how he speaks when you talk with him, and how he writes if he gives you material he's drafted. As I mentioned, during phone conversations, I make notes of phrases and expressions my client uses, his word choices, preferred sentence structure (i.e., short, snappy sentences, or long, rambling ones?), the way he speaks. I want him to read the book and think, "Wow—this sounds just like me."

Robertson has found that a face-to-face meeting makes a big difference in nailing the way a person talks—and thinks. "I'm trying to get a feel for how they talk and what their personality is and what their passions are," says Robertson. "I like to meet in person so I can get a feel for their voice. Then the sitting down and writing part is done through email and phone calls."

Robertson, who has co-written memoirs, says he thinks of himself as a frustrated novelist. "To tell someone else's story, you have to think like that person, capture his persona and personality. It's like assuming the life of a character you're creating in a novel," he explains. "To do that, especially if I'm starting from scratch, it's really helpful to spend as much face time as possible."

Turner agrees meeting someone in person makes it easier to capture a client's unique way of speaking and writing. "I'd never met any of my clients until a couple of years ago, and I was surprised to see how much it helped with her voice," says Turner. "Just hearing how she spoke and the words she used and how she approached things really helped with the voice and the book."

Getting What You Need

Consider the easiest way to get the information you need from your client. Some clients like to write material for you (this is my preference!); others will prefer that you interview them. I try to do these types of interviews by phone to save time; you can use Skype or FaceTime to elicit more information (body language, mannerisms, etc.) during these calls.

"For clients who prefer phone interviews, I type what they say into a Word document as they speak," says Graciela Sholander. "I'm a fast typist so this usually works well for me—better than recording and transcribing the audio, which I find tedious. Admittedly, my method works best with clients who speak at a slower, even pace. My preferred method, however, is to have one or two initial phone conversations to get the gist of the project and catch more of the voice and personality of the client, followed by primarily email communication thereafter through the life of the project."

Whether I'm writing my own book or a client's, I use a fairly simple system to stay organized. I use manila folders, label them with chapter numbers, and put any relevant information in each folder. I also create a folder in Word where I keep all documents relating to the book, and create a special folder in Outlook so my client's emails are in one place.

"Whether it's your own book or a client's, you have to stay organized," says Turner, who also uses separate folders for each chapter of a project. "You'll come across info that you think is relevant and unless you put it somewhere where you can find it again, you're going to waste hours and hours looking for it, and that may make the difference in your book."

Ghostwriter as Therapist

In addition to project manager and writer, there's an unexpected role you may play with your client—therapist. Many of your clients will never have written a book before. They may be intimidated by the process, nervous about working with a ghostwriter, or worried that you'll "take over" their book.

"Most people are anxious," says Stephanie Golden. "Right now I'm editing the memoirs of an ex-congressman and he was afraid I would butcher his book and take away all of his precious anecdotes. The first thing to working successfully is to understand that clients are anxious. Don't forget that."

You don't need to hold their hands all the time but I want my client to feel confident and excited, not overwhelmed, about the process. How do I do that?

- I always refer to the book as "your book" even if I'm working as a coauthor, with my name on the cover. This is a subtle but effective reminder for the client, who may be nervous about not having *his* vision come through.
- I always tell the client to let me know if he has questions...and when we speak by phone, end each call with an open-ended question like "Is there anything else on your mind I should know about?" or "How do you feel about how we're progressing?" You'd be surprised...even the most successful businessperson may have what he thinks is a "dumb" question, and this gives him permission to ask it.
- I *listen* to the client, and make sure that I understand what he's telling me by reflecting back the message he's communicating. I always want to make sure we're on the same page, pardon the pun.
- If I'm asked for my opinion, I offer it. Otherwise, I try to give objective advice and let the client make the big and small decisions about the book.
- I write the best book I can, but I give the credit to the client. This is his baby, not mine. (Yes, I know the book wouldn't exist without my amazing talent...but I keep that to myself.)

You may have been hired for your writing skills, but let me tell you something—your ability to treat a client with respect, patience, and even compassion will resonate with that person long after you finish his book.

Drafts and Disagreements: How to Handle Them

I like to work by sending one chapter at a time to the client for his review. Then he returns the document to me with any edits or requested changes. If they're minor, I just review them and move on; if there are substantial or numerous changes, however, I schedule a brief phone interview to discuss them. I take notes during that call and rewrite the chapter per the client's comments afterwards. That gives us a chance to actually discuss why a client doesn't like a particular section and talk about it as opposed to trying to "read between the lines" with email.

See, I always want to know why the client isn't happy with something before I change or tweak it. For example, one of my clients had written a memoir about his work founding and running several nonprofits. He hired me to work as a developmental editor to improve the book.

In the first chapter, the client had spent a lot of time describing how he met and fell in love with his wife—too much time, in my opinion. I cut a lot of the story and tightened the rest, and then explained that I thought that the back story was dragging the pace down, and that readers wouldn't care as much as he did about how wonderful his wife was. (And she is—I've met her!) After hearing me out, he agreed to take my approach.

In other cases, though, the client will insist on including material I think is extraneous or distracting, and that's up to him. I will state my opinion, and why, but the final say is his. Then I make those changes and send the final version of the chapter to my client to sign off on—and we're onto the next one. Once all of the chapters are done (or the sections of the book proposal are complete), I create one document that includes everything— the final draft—and send it to my client for final review.

After he signs off on the completed manuscript and sends my last check, we're done—unless he hires me again for another project. I always send a thank-you note, and I'm also happy to answer brief questions that may crop up after the book is published. I look at that as relationship-maintenance and don't charge for it—unless it starts to eat up a lot of time.

Then I'll suggest charging an hourly consulting rate. But I've found that taking the time with a client even after my paying work has been completed is good karma and gratifying for me. And you know what else? It makes my client happy, and makes him more likely to recommend me to friends and colleagues—which is excellent news for my business in the future.

Chapter 10

Trouble-Shooting: Addressing Common Ghosting Problems

Regardless of whether you do content marketing for corporate clients or ghostwrite books for individuals, you're likely to face some challenges during the researching and writing process. If you've written professionally, you know that's part of freelancing. You can't get in touch with a critical source for an article. Your editor pushes up a deadline. You start writing a piece with a specific premise per your editor, only to discover that the premise isn't supported by current research.

Ghostwriting, especially longer pieces, multiples the issues that may arise. After all, the idea for the book or blog post or article didn't spring from the creative recesses of *your* brain. It came from your client's. That may make it more challenging to deliver the type of piece your client is envisioning, at least at first. However, if you get a foothold working for a particular client doing content marketing or ghosting blog posts, for example, you'll start generating ideas for possible pieces because you've immersed yourself in the subject to do a good job for your client. As I mentioned earlier, that makes you more valuable to your client—and helps you work more quickly too.

But with any assignment, whether ghostwritten or not, it comes down to several basic factors:

1. You talk to the client or editor about what he or she wants.
2. You write the piece (whether it's a book chapter, a blog post, an article) and hand it off to your client.
3. Your client is happy with the work—and pays you for it. On time.

Sounds simple, doesn't it? Yet no matter how talented, diligent, and professional you are, you'll likely face certain issues as a ghost. Paraphrasing Louis Pasteur, "luck favors the prepared mind." In other words, take a look at common problems that arise when ghostwriting, talk about how to avoid them if you can—and address and overcome them if you cannot.

Problem: Client Won't Pay

I've listed this one first because if you want to make money as a ghost, you've got to be paid for your work. Clients sometimes don't pay, or don't pay on time. They may start the project full of enthusiasm and drive, and then lose interest. Or they may face a change in financial circumstances. Or they may just "forget" about paying you. (Yeah, right.)

This is why I suggest you get a retainer upfront for anything except the very shortest assignments. That protects your initial investment of time and work. An agreed-to schedule for payment **in writing** will also help ensure that you get your money when you're supposed to. (It's smart to have a provision in your contract that provides that if the contract is terminated, you'll be paid for any work already performed.) "I structure payment schedules tied to milestones," says Gwen Moran. "I'm unable to move to the next milestone until we complete that part of the project and it's paid [for]."

But what if your client stops paying in the middle of a project? First, remind him, and give him an opportunity to pay. If he still doesn't, give him one last deadline—and then terminate the relationship. You need to get out of a bad situation and move on to clients who *will* pay you. Protect your time, and your business.

Problem: Client is Unavailable

At some point, you're going need access to your client, even if it's just having him read and review your work. What happens if he falls off the proverbial face of the earth?

To avoid this, make sure your client understands at the outset the importance of his involvement, whether it's providing information or being interviewed or reviewing your work. If he doesn't give you what you need, you won't be able to write the book.

"This is probably my biggest challenge. I work with many busy executives. They're often traveling extensively and have great demands on their time. Even when you're working with a ghostwriter, a book is a tremendous time commitment," says Gwen Moran. "The ghost may write the words, but the content and ideas have to come from the client's head. So, I try to gather any background in advance and always work from an extensive outline. I'll schedule calls and talk through the chapter with the client, recording and transcribing our session so I have as much material as possible to work with. I usually schedule the next interview while I have the client on the phone, so we have another mini-deadline. I'll also send questions by email."

Even that doesn't ensure that your client will stay on track, however. Marcia Layton Turner recently had a project where the author got so busy the project stalled. "I have no control over when it's going to get restarted and we're halfway through," she says. "I know he wants to get it wrapped up but I'm sort of at his mercy. What I learned from that is to put some timelines and consequences in the contract to put the onus on the author to keep it moving."

Even for shorter work, you're likely to need client input at some point. For example, I was ghosting an article for a client and had several questions for her that had to be answered before I could finish the initial draft. If they had been minor details, I would have sent it to her with TKs and asked for the information. But these questions were more involved, so I needed to connect with my client, even if only through email. If I have a slew of questions, I'll often schedule a phone call as that is often quicker than sending longwinded emails back and forth—and it's easier for the client, too.

Problem: Client Is *Too* Available

I've found this to be more of an issue with the EJs, or Everyday Joes, than other types of clients. If you're working with a high-powered business exec, for example, he has much more on his plate than his book project. But other clients will want to touch base constantly—and every time interruption takes time away from your work.

"You may need to establish boundaries," says Sondra Forsyth. "Even the most grateful of experts, the ones who are properly awed by your genius and your way with words, can drive you crazy unless you agree on a few rules." Like me, she suggests that her authors use email to set up phone appointments so she can work without frequent "helpful" interruptions.

But if you're dealing with busy clients, especially PPs, you may have to make some concessions and be available when they are. "I won't accept calls at all hours, but I will make myself available to accommodate a client's schedule. So, if a Saturday or evening phone call is necessary, I have no problem with that. But I can't accommodate multiple calls in a week unless there are extenuating circumstances, such as a project that has a very fast turnaround," says Gwen Moran. "I have to be able to manage my work and my life. If one client is demanding more than the scope of work we've defined, that becomes disruptive to my overall time management structure and something has to give. Often, though, when this happens, it's just a case of nerves or exuberance on the client's part. It usually takes one conversation to reset expectations and get things back on track."

Problem: You Have More Than One Boss

When you ghostwrite for one client, you have one person to make happy. If you're hired by an editor, agent, or business, though, you must determine just *who* you have to please, and whether there's more than one person who will be signing off on your work. For example, I wrote a book proposal for a client but then had to rework it per his agent's input—something I hadn't anticipated at the outset. I don't mind working for more than one boss, but I want to know that going in.

Turner had a corporate client where a committee was responsible for reviewing the book. "I would write chapters, send it the committee, we'd have a conference call, and I'd make changes. The president didn't start reading the chapters until halfway through," says Turner. Alas, the president didn't like the book's approach and pulled the plug on the project.

"I don't think anything could have been done—there was a difference in opinion in the way the book was going to go," she adds. "But the lesson is that you want to make sure that the decision-maker is reading along and commenting on it."

The more people you have to please, the more difficult it may be to get them to agree on the actual book content, too, points out Kathi Ann Brown. "History is by nature 'political'—whether it's a corporate history or a family history. Rarely will you work on a project that doesn't involve some measure of controversy, sensitivity, and disagreement, if only because people remember and value the past differently," says Brown. "One person's 'truth' is another person's 'fairy tale.' I lean on documents to get the facts and on people to get the story behind the facts."

"It's important to be a good researcher," agrees Heidi Tyline King. "Don't just take the CEO's word for it—unless it's supposed to be coming from the mouth of the CEO and that's how he wants it."

However, even due diligence may not protect you. Recently I wrote a book for a client who already had a publishing contract. My contract was a side agreement with her, not the publisher itself. We worked well together and she was very happy with my work. Then she submitted a couple of chapters to her editor, who requested some changes in tone and structure.

Fine. I rewrote them, and my client turned them in again. Then a second editor got into the game, and requested a complete rewrite according to *his* changes.

My point? I wound up doing a lot more rewriting than I ever expected, because I didn't realize I would have three people—with three very different approaches—to please.

Problem: Client Fancies Himself a Writer

This is a tricky one. Some clients are actually excellent writers and their work just needs a little tuning up. In fact, some of my "ghosting" gigs could actually be considered in-depth editing jobs. You say "poe-tae-toe," I say, "po-tah-to;" it doesn't matter to me what you call what I'm doing for you, as long as you pay me fairly for it.

Alas, I've found some clients believe themselves to possess exemplary writing skills—but they do not. Take the client who provided me with a 700-page "book" that only needed some editing to make it publishable. At least that's what he said. Well, he didn't give me a 700-page book. He gave me a 700-page collection of notes, scientific research findings, and rambling insights that he had worked on for several years. He thought it was a book; no one had ever told him otherwise.

But what he gave me was the background I needed to write a book proposal for him. I also used the "sandwich" approach to let him know that what he had wasn't appropriate for publication. (To sandwich something, you start with a compliment, slide the criticism or negative comment in the middle, and slap another compliment or nice comment on top.) I said something like, "I'm very impressed with the depth and amount of research you've done already, but we will need to take this information and rework it so an everyday person can read and understand it. It will take some time, but I'm very excited about working with you to make that happen and make your work accessible to the public."

Get the idea? No matter what you're ghosting, let your client know you appreciate his efforts (even if they're not up to par), and don't bash your client's work. If your client provides you with written material for your project, edit it, revise it, tweak it—do what you need to make it work. Over time, savvy clients will figure out that their words need some help, and will often even tell you to go ahead and "make it sound good."

Problem: Client Wants You to Do More Work

In some ways, this is to be expected when you're working for a set fee—we all tend to want more than what we pay for. "It's almost human nature—people will try to suck more out of you," says Melanie Votaw. "I'll put in contract parameters when I work with a flat fee. People will say, 'oh, it will only take you an hour or two,' but everyone asks you to do it!"

I call this "work creep," and it does happen often. If I'm charging a client by the hour, I don't mind so much—after all, I'm going to be paid for what I do. But I've gotten much better about figuring out what the project includes—and doesn't—at the outset.

"My agreements are pretty detailed in defining the scope of work. If the project begins to creep beyond that, I've already worked out a compensation plan for that," says Moran. "But, again, it's critical to keep communicating and managing expectations. No one wants to be hit with an extra fee because he or she lost track of how many revisions have been done. I never up-charge a client without a heads-up…that we're moving beyond the original scope of work."

I look at it this way. The first draft of a piece is that—a first draft. I expect some edits and changes; I'm making an educated, informed guess (thanks to what I've gleaned from the client) about what he wants. After he gives me feedback, I rework the piece and send it back to him for his review and approval. A few minor changes to the second draft? Fine.

But at that point, I'm ready to be done. And I've had clients who want to continually tinker with the work, or decide to add something new to it, or worse yet, take an entirely new approach. That becomes a problem. Make sure your contract specifies the amount of work you're performing, and that the client understands that as well.

Problem: You Disagree with Your Client

This is one of the most common issues that arise during the ghosting process. At some point, your client will disagree with your approach. It could be word choice, organization, or overall tone. That's where your skill as an arbiter comes in. As a ghost, you've got to be able to take criticism, understand why the client isn't pleased, and negotiate some kind of compromise that will make your client happy. That doesn't mean you have to be a doormat, but you do have to be able to disagree without burning bridges.

Tim Gower learned this lesson early on. "With my first project, I submitted the first chunk of text to the author for his approval," says Gower. "He sent it back to me with the entire first page X-ed out and then rewrote it in his own voice, completely changing the message. I was so angry I went out and ran five miles."

After he cooled off—literally and figuratively—Gower spoke with his client, explaining why he didn't think the client's approach would work for the book. "There was an education process for both of us" says Gower. "He had to learn about what a consumer would expect, and I had to appreciate his level of scientific sophistication."

Usually the more input your client has, the less work the book is for you—and the happier your client will be with the finished project. "Some coauthors like to make changes in the documents themselves," says Forsyth. "As long as 'Track Changes' is on, this method is not a problem for me because I can find the interpolated sections easily and fix any grammar goofs or smooth out transitions. Other coauthors prefer to call me to discuss changes. That's fine, too. In most cases, input from my coauthors is helpful rather than annoying!"

Problem: Client's Not Happy with Your Work

Yes, it happens. Despite your efforts, the client isn't happy. Then it's your job to find out precisely what your client isn't happy about. I turned in an article to a client who was new to me, and she emailed back to say she didn't like how I'd approached the topic, but she didn't give me any guidance about what she wanted.

Once again, this isn't an exchange you want to have via email. Here's what I wrote back to her:

> Dear Roberta:
>
> Thanks for your email and for getting back to me so quickly; I appreciate it. I'm sorry to learn that you're not happy with how I approached the article. Are you available to talk sometime today? I'd like to talk to you about the article so I can rework it and give you what you want—that's my job, after all!
>
> Thanks very much and I look forward to speaking with you soon.
>
> Sincerely,
> Kelly

Note the tone of my email? As the saying goes, you catch more flies with honey than vinegar. The client and I connected later that day, and she told me that she had expected a more academic tone than I had written. I reworked the article, turned it in the next day, and she was happy with it.

Often it's a question of not capturing the client's voice, or letting your own voice as a writer overtake the book. "I made some mistakes early on where I infused too much of my personality into the story," says Robertson. "I paid the price in the short term as I lost the project, but I benefited in the long term as I learned not to do that."

Remember too that even if you think your approach is the right one, as a ghostwriter, you're working for your client. You have to be able to set your ego aside and let your client's story and voice come through. "You have to have a certain disposition to do this," says Robertson. "Everyone has an ego. To do this successfully, you have to set it aside you are the vessel with which someone is entrusting you to tell *their* story."

Heidi Tyline King provides clients with the first finished chapter so they can review it for content, tone and style before she writes the rest of the book. She then turns in the completed manuscript for final review. However, many ghostwriters (myself included) like to work chapter by chapter. That keeps the client involved throughout the process and prevents big unhappy surprises at the end.

Problem: Client Won't Let You Finish

I haven't found this to be an issue with shorter pieces. Usually your client has a deadline in mind, whether it's to submit an article to a trade magazine or to get some content up, and he's motivated to get the piece done already. But that's not always the case when you're ghosting a book. Sure, *you* want to actually complete the book, collect your final check, and move on to the next assignment. But what happens when your client keeps coming up with material he wants to include in earlier (and supposedly finished) chapters? (This is what I call the OMTs, for "One More Thing," and it's a fairly common affliction among ghosting clients.)

In one instance, I was writing a book for a client who worked in the media. She kept close tabs on research in her subject area, and continually sent me emails of studies, press releases, and news stories she thought would work for the book. That was great at the outset, but as we progressed, I had to explain that I couldn't keep going back to chapters we'd finished to add new material.

Every time I did so, it took me time—time that took away from writing the remaining chapters and meeting our publisher's deadline. I also explained that a book, by its nature, is somewhat static. Once it's published, unless you update it, that's it. So at some point, you have to say, "Okay—we are done."

That approach worked with her. But to avoid this problem, you need to be clear about what your scope of work is, and how many rewrites you'll provide before you charge for them. (See, Problem: Client Wants You to do More Work, earlier in this chapter.) I have no problem going back to add an anecdote or fact in an earlier chapter—after all, sometimes you'll stumble across something while writing chapter 11 that should be referred to or included in chapter 4 or 5. But this should be the exception, not the rule.

Problem: You're *Done* with This Client

What happens when despite your best efforts, you simply can't make a project work? Then it may be time to cut bait and move on.

"I haven't fired many clients, but on occasion, a project just isn't working out and it's in everyone's best interest to part ways. Again, I usually have clear milestones, so I do my best to make it to the next milestone and then have a discussion about why the project isn't working out," says Moran. "If we can't resolve it, I have said that it might be best for the client to find another writer. But, honestly, most clients are professionals and we're able to work together to bring the project to a successful conclusion."

If you do have a situation where you decide to walk away, keep it professional. Tell the client why you're terminating the relationship (e.g., failure to pay, failure to provide you with needed information, failure to treat you with respect), and wish them luck in the future—without telling them they'll need it. Chalk it up to one more lesson you've learned as a ghostwriter, and start looking for your next project.

Problem: You Have to Rewrite

If you've written for publication before, you've no doubt been through the rewrite mill. My least favorite thing for an editor to say (well, after "we're going out of business and wont' be able to pay you the $3,000 we owe you.") is something like, "Well, you've got a great start here, but..." Then the pause. Or "this piece just isn't working for me." Or I've read through your article and it needs some work."

Any statement along these lines means it's rewrite time. And I hate rewrites for several reasons.

First, nearly all of my work, whether ghostwritten or not, is paid on a per-word (articles) or per-project (such as with a ghosted book proposal, book, or blog post of a certain number of words). That figure, divided by the number of hours it takes to complete the project, represents my hourly rate. So if the project for the court reporter client takes four hours (which was what I estimated, including one rewrite), I'm looking at an hourly rate of $100. Not bad—and in fact, it's what I try to average as a ghostwriter and journalist, especially now that I work part-time.

Now assume that the project takes longer—say six hours. My hourly rate has now dropped to $75. And if I have to rewrite multiple times, and for some reason it takes eight hours, then I'm at $50/hour.

Get the idea? In short, the more rewrites you do, the lower your hourly rate becomes.

That's the first problem. The second is that when you're rewriting a piece for one client, you're unable to work for other clients. That's called opportunity cost. Third, and not to be overlooked, is that darn PIA factor. Once I write something, I want to have it done. I don't want to rewrite it, and rewrite it, and rewrite it. I want to turn it in, get paid, and move on. Rewrites prevent me from doing so.

Yet as a ghost, some rewriting is a given. You may capture your client's voice and the substance of the piece on your first try. Or you may not. Remember that I always plan on a three-draft process and I expect rewrites. Do the same thing as a ghost and you'll minimize the stress on yourself.

Problem: Client Wants You to Write *and* Place the Piece

Some of your ghosting clients may be savvy about the publishing industry, but let's assume most are not. So you may run into the issue of when a client wants you to write an article for him, and place it as well, meaning that you pitch the piece to a publication to hopefully get it into print or published online.

There are several problems with this. First, you are a ghostwriter, not a PR pro. When you work in public relations, your job is to get media coverage for your client. As a ghostwriter, your job is to write. Yes, you want to write well, and in the voice of your client, and to meet the needs of the market if he has one in mind. But it's outside your "scope of work" to ensure that anything you write gets published.

In addition to being outside what you're paid to do, there's an ethical quandary as well. You can't be paid by two different clients—a market and your ghostwriting client—for the same work. Make sure that your clients understand this, and that your job is to write, not to place.

Problem: You Lack Clips

Ghostwriters write without a byline, and often with no acknowledgement at all. So how do you create a portfolio that you can use with potential clients? First, don't be afraid to ask for permission from a client to use samples of work. (I often include a provision in ghostwriting contracts that addressing this issue.) I've found most clients are willing to allow this, as long as you're not posting their work on your website or otherwise publicizing the fact that you wrote it.

Other clients, however, particularly celebrities will have a vested interest in protecting the fact that you didn't actually write their books, and will insist on an NDA (non-disclosure agreement) which precludes you from telling anyone about your work. In this case, you can still say something like, "I've written a memoir for a young actress for a major publisher," without identifying your client—and that credit should help you get other work.

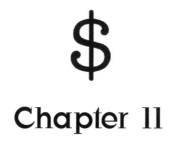

Chapter 11

Ghostwriter, Revealed:

Making it Work

In the preceding chapters, you've learned about how to market yourself, evaluate clients, negotiate fees, and work efficiently as a ghostwriter or coauthor. This chapter, we'll talk about making your business work both day to day.

The Magical, Mythical Work Balance

What's work balance? Having just enough work, but not too much, at all times. That means you're busy but not overwhelmed, chugging along productively without becoming derailed by too much work—or too much downtime. And let me tell you something as a self-employed business person with 16+ years of experience—work balance is a myth.

Yes, there are times when I have just the right amount of work. I put in the hours I want, average the hourly rate I aim for ($100/hour), and finish assignments in the time I've allotted for work. As I finish one big project, another appears in the wings. I'm like a well-oiled machine, working efficiently and with a minimum of stress.

Those times are—well, if not rare, they're not common. Usually I have a bit too much work or not quite enough. That's the struggle as a freelancer and that includes working as a ghostwriter. You don't have a boss to hand you assignments—you've got to be out there beating the proverbial bushes for work as you are actually working on your current projects. Otherwise, when you finish a book or other big project, you may discover that you have nothing lined up. It's one thing to take planned time off— that's called vacation. But unexpected "dead time" can undermine your business, as well as your emotional health.

Let me tell you, when I don't have enough work, I'm not skipping around, smug in the knowledge that *something* will come my way. I freak out...at least a little...and then start worrying that my business will tank because I haven't been aggressive enough with my marketing.

Because I work a limited number of hours, I only work on one book for a client at a time. And each book is a sizable project that hopefully pays a significant amount of money. But unfortunately, another juicy book project doesn't just happen to drop into my lap as I finish the first one. There's almost always a lag between big assignments.

That's why I always keep a mix of work irons in the fire. At any given time, I want to have at least one ghosting project, be it a book or book proposal, going on. I'm also writing articles for a variety of magazines. I'm doing occasional speaking gigs. I'm teaching online and in-person classes. I'm selling reprints, and syndicating other writers' work to a custom magazine publisher. I may be working on my own book, or promoting my own titles that are already in print.

Other successful ghosts take a similar approach. "I work on my own books, client's books, articles, and corporate projects. I'll typically have several different kinds of projects going on at once," says Gwen Moran. "Books, big articles or other heavily researched projects, and shorter pieces each have different cycles. I like having a mix so that I can always use my time productively. Short-turnaround projects provide more instant writing gratification and cash flow while longer-term projects provide a different kind of satisfaction and allow me to have more extensive projects to fill my time."

Melanie Votaw also likes to have multiple projects on her desk at any given time to help maintain a steady workload. "There's always the possibility of the delay factor," she explains. "I don't like having just one project—it makes me nervous." In addition to ghostwriting, Votaw does copywriting, editing, and article writing for a balance of different types of work.

How much work you can handle will depend on factors like the complexity and length of the projects, your energy level, and how many hours you put in. I aim to ghost or coauthor two books a year in addition to the rest of my freelance work. Jill Amadio can ghostwrite two books a year; three if they're 50,000-word business books. Because of the extensive amount of research involved, Heidi Tyline King prefers to do one corporate history at a time. "I have done two at a time, and about five years ago, I had three books going and tons of articles," says King. "It was great money but I just about killed myself."

Marcia Layton Turner has done as many as four books at a time, with each at a different stage. "Right now, I have one that is almost done, and a proposal that I'm starting but I also like to have the shorter magazine assignments because I like variety," says Turner. "And if I was only working on a book, I'd get bored. I like the immediate gratification of getting something done, and getting a check."

In addition to running CorporateHistory.net, Marian Calabro teaches and writes her own book. Yet she says her primary responsibility as a business owner is to get new clients. "Although I don't think of myself as a salesperson, indeed my main task is to sell," says Calabro. "No new projects, no work."

That's the other part of the work picture you have to balance. The work I do (writing articles, selling reprints, writing my own books, and speaking) all contribute to my bottom line, and help me survive those periods when I don't have a ghosting gig. But in addition to paying work, I have to devote time to marketing my ghostwriting business, looking for new clients, qualifying them, and hopefully getting them to hire me. In any given week, that may include:

- Blogging about successful freelancing, whether on my own blog or posting on writing-related blogs;
- Searching CraigsList.org and other websites for potential ghosting gigs and sending out LOIs;
- Checking the websites of organizations like ASJA and the Association of Ghostwriters for job postings and sending LOIs;
- Responding to requests from potential clients for more information about what I do; and
- Following up on leads who may need or know someone who needs a ghostwriter.

Just remember that while this marketing is crucial for the success of my business, it doesn't pay off unless and until I actually get a paying client out of it. The fact that it takes more time and effort to land a ghosting book client as opposed to, say, getting an article assignment from a magazine editor, means that I have to take a long-view approach to marketing my business.

Yes, I've had clients hire me within a day or two of contacting me. But usually it takes time—time to send an LOI, time to talk with the client, time to review material and create a bid, time for the client to review my bid and decide to hire me, and time to negotiate the final fee. That's another reason to keep up magazine work or other writing that has a quicker turnaround.

"Several years ago I did two books back to back and stopped querying magazines for the duration. Big mistake!" says Sondra Forsyth. "By the time I was ready to get back to article writing, the editorial game of musical chairs had left me with not one familiar name on the mastheads of my former markets." While Forsyth eventually started getting assignments again, two magazines started her at newcomer rates even though she'd previously been making top dollar.

"After that eye-opener, I've made a practice of continuing to write for magazines even when I'm working on a book," says Forsyth. "This tactic turns out to be easier than I had thought it would be. Taking a break from a book project while I meet article deadlines means that I go back to the manuscript with a fresh perspective and renewed enthusiasm."

And never count your chickens before they're hatched—no matter how promising a client may sound, until you sign him, and you do the work and get paid in full, there is no guarantee that things will proceed as you've planned. "Having work you've counted on fall through is probably the most frustrating aspect of ghostwriting," says Votaw. "I just had a project that was going to be my big summer project fall through and suddenly I had to scramble. I had expected to have $5,000 in my pocket, but he's a procrastinator and I just couldn't get him to do it."

That's the thing—you can lose a project through no fault of your own. That's why you should always be in hustle mode when it comes to getting more work. So, no matter how busy I am, I get back to potential clients immediately. I don't want to lose out on what could be a lucrative gig because the client wound up choosing the first person who responded. An EJ may contact only you, but agents, editors, and PPs will usually be considering a number of possible ghostwriters for any given gig. Why not get first in line (or close) when you can?

Track Your Minutes, Boost Your Hourly Rate

In chapter 6, you learned about the different ways to charge (per-hour, per-project, and per-word). Yet knowing how long a project will take takes experience. I'm a fan of tracking the time I put in on book, even if I'm working for a set fee, so I can tell later what my hourly rate was for the project. That helps me determine whether it was truly worthwhile, and helps me set fees in the future.

We talked about hourly rates in chapter 1, but let's revisit the subject once more. Remember that I started out as a freelance writer doing most of my work for magazines, where you're paid a per-word rate. And I've seen a lot of writers get hung up on per-word rates. Under some writers' logic, a magazine that pays $2/word must be twice as good as a $1/word market, and four times as good as a market that pays only $0.50/word.

But that's often not the case. Recall that markets that pay less than $1/word (currently the majority of my regular magazine work) produce a higher per-hour rate for me because the stories take less time to pitch, are assigned more quickly, are more straightforward, and receive fewer requests for revisions. In fact, your per-hour rate is often the strongest indicator of your productivity whether you're writing for a magazine, a ghosting client, or a book publisher.

At this point in my career, my goal is to average $100/hour. I keep that figure in mind when I'm bidding on work. (An aside: don't feel bad if that figure sounds ambitious to you. Remember that I work part-time hours, averaging about 15/week. I have two little kids at home and work part-time by choice, so my hourly rate has to stay high for me to make what I want in a limited amount of time.)

What's your average hourly rate? You can't answer that question unless you know how you're spending your time. When I was a lawyer, I had to keep track of what I did during the day because that's how my firm billed clients—by the hour. That habit spilled over into my freelancing business. While I don't track every single minute (I don't want to know how much time I waste on Facebook!), I usually have a good idea of how I'm spending my time—and how long different types of assignments take me to complete.

For some projects, you may already be charging by the hour. Otherwise you can track your time by jotting it down or using software like Traxtime. Keeping records of every task you do while you're working on an assignment may reveal that you're not working as efficiently as you thought—or that your hourly rate is higher than you realized. Here's an example for a book proposal that paid $3,500:

11.09.09	Review client material: 2.5 hours
11.10.09	Review material/start draft: 2.0 hours
11.12.09	Draft overview/start marketing: 1.75 hours
11.15.09	Research for comp. analysis: 1.50 hours
11.16.09	Comp. analysis, marketing stuff: 2.0 hours
11.18.09	Research/chapter summaries: 2.0 hours
11.19.09	Chapter summaries/research: 2.5 hours
11.21.09	Start sample chapter/summaries: 2.25 hours
11.23.09	Sample chapter: 2.5 hours

11.24.09	Pull together proposal: 1.75 hours
11.30.09	Proof/finish proposal/to client: 1.25 hours
12.03.09	Phonecon with client/start edits: 1.25 hours
12.06.09	Final draft, proof, to client: 1.75 hours

TOTAL: 25 hours

For this book proposal, I put in 25 hours, including research and was paid a flat fee of $3,500. That translates into $140/hour, an excellent rate. (I don't always make that much, believe me!) This particular client had a lot of material and research to draw from, which made the proposal relatively easy to write—I had estimated that it would take at least 10 hours' longer than it did.

The point is to stay aware of how long projects take you so you can keep tabs on your hourly rate even when you're receiving a flat fee. I suggest you take a similar approach—and always strive to either boost your hourly rate, work as efficiently as possible, or both.

Building your Business: Make Clients Love You

One of the easiest ways to boost your hourly rate is to do more work for your current clients. That cuts your marketing time, which means you have more hours to spend writing for money. There's another aspect to turning a "one-shot" client into a regular one—and clients who are happy with your work are more likely to recommend you to other potential clients. When new clients come to you, you cut your marketing time even further. (It's worth noting that at this point in my career more than 80 percent of my work comes from referrals, as opposed to the work I find on my own. Most experienced ghostwriters find that at least half of their work comes from referrals and recommendations.)

So how do you make clients love you? It's not that difficult if you follow the Golden Rule ("Treat others the way you would like to be treated.") and keep these five tips in mind:

1. *Do what you say you will.* I'm always surprised by writers who miss deadlines, or sources who aren't available when I call to perform a prearranged interview. How hard is it to follow through on your word? If you tell a client you'll have a piece to her for her review by noon on Friday, then you email it to her by then—preferably earlier! And if for some reason you cannot, let the client know as soon as you realize you won't be able to do what you promised. You want

your client to trust and respect you, and in my opinion, that starts with her being able to rely on you.

2. *Stay in touch!* You needn't pepper a client with emails or texts (and in fact, constant contact drives me crazy.) But if you're working on a big project, it's smart to touch base every week or so to tell your client what's happening. It doesn't matter whether you have several clients or a dozen that you're currently writing for; each client should feel like your priority and keeping her in the loop will be appreciated.

3. *Compliment when you can.* People like to feel like they're appreciated. And they like to be noticed. Give your client some positive strokes when you can. Maybe she's written a stellar description of an incident that helps you with a chapter you're working on, or her suggested edits have made an article easier for readers to grasp. Let her know! As poet Maya Angelou said, "people may not remember what you said, but they will always remember how you made them *feel.*"

4. *Be gracious.* You're competing against thousands of other ghostwriters every day. What sets you apart? Hopefully your talent, your dedication, and your knowledge (and willingness to learn about) of what you're writing about. But don't overlook the importance of being, well, nice. When someone refers a new client to me, I send a personal note to him to say thank you. I think it's important to be gracious with people (including clients); that helps me stand out from the competition out there.

5. *Let it slide.* As the saying goes, "stuff happens." It's not always good stuff. In the last few months, I've lost out on three lucrative ghosting projects, two of which I thought I was perfect for. In the meantime, I'm chasing down money another client owes me and trying to sign another client who may or may not turn out to be a bit of a control freak. But you know what? That's all part of this business. Take a few minutes— an evening if you must—to vent, rant, complain, or bitch to a trusted friend or fellow writer who "gets it." And then start the next morning with a positive attitude and let the crap slide, so to speak.

One More Bonus of Ghosting

With this book in hand, you have the basic information, strategies, and templates to help you launch, build, and maintain a successful ghostwriting business. I'd like to leave you with one last thought—the sometimes overlooked gratification of ghostwriting if you decide to pursue book projects.

Don't get me wrong—you can stick with creating shorter pieces for clients and have a successful ghosting career. But to me, ghostwriting books is even more satisfying. While I've written more than 1,000 articles for national magazines and reprinted three times that in more than 100 publications of all sizes, I can tell you that articles pale when it comes to writing a book.

A book has weight. A book has heft. A book—well, a book *matters*. Maybe not to everyone, but it matters a lot to its author. It matters to its readers. A book can make a difference in a reader's life—it can spur a person to action, teach him something he needed to learn, change the way he thinks about a topic, even change the person he is.

The ability to conceptualize, research, and write the 40,000, 50,000, or 75,000 words that comprise a book is impressive. Despite the six million Americans who have already written books (or at least claim to), most people can't do it. The ability to write for someone else—to channel your client's ideas and concept into an actual book that will last for decades, even centuries—is an even rarer skill. If you're able to do it and do it well, you'll find that a career as a ghostwriter pays both financial and psychic rewards. When a client calls and says, "Kelly, I'm sitting here, holding my book in my hands," and I hear the excitement in his voice, I'm delighted to share that experience with him.

Remember I didn't intend to ghostwrite or coauthor when I launched my freelance career—I was only interested in writing my own books. I'm so grateful to have had the epiphany years later when I realized that writing other people's books could be more lucrative for me financially. I had no idea of the emotional satisfaction I'd get from helping a client get the book he dreams of writing out of his head and onto the page.

I think that's why so many ghosts stay in the business once they get into it. Even I will admit that it's not just about the money. It's about the work, the challenge, and the satisfaction. "I love every step of the process: finding good material, figuring out what's valuable and why, keeping track of it all, assembling a good story, and then putting it into pretty prose," says Kathi Ann Brown. "And, naturally, seeing my client's face light up when they open 'their' book for the first time."

"Ghosting has been a rewarding way to make a living on many levels and I've had some wonderful clients. For me, it's been an important part of building a diversified and sustainable writing business," says Moran. "I love being able to help people tell their stories and get their ideas out into the world. Publishing a book is a dream for many people, and it feels great to help bring that dream to reality."

I couldn't agree more. No matter how you choose to approach ghostwriting, I hope you'll consider making this lucrative niche part of your freelancing reality—and that the reality exceeds your dreams.

Get in Touch—and Stay in Touch

First, thanks so much for buying this book! I hope it helps you break into the ghostwriting field, and make more money as a writer! If you have a question you didn't find addressed in the preceding pages or just want to say "hi," drop me a note at Kelly@becomebodywise.com and you'll hear back from me. In the meantime, check out my blog, http://dollarsanddeadlines.blogspot.com, which helps nonfiction writers make more money in less time.

Want to know more about me? Let's see: I "escaped from the law" in 1997, leaving my former life as an attorney to launch a successful freelance career, writing more than 1,000 articles for more than 60 national magazines. I'm known as a freelancing expert and my books include *Six-Figure Freelancing: The Writer's Guide to Making More Money, Second Edition* and *Dollars and Deadlines: Make Money Writing Articles for Print and Online Markets*. I'm also a seasoned ghostwriter and coauthor and my collaborative books include *Small Changes, Big Results, Revised and Updated: A Wellness Plan with 65 Recipes* (with Ellie Krieger, R.D.).

In addition to ghostwriting, authoring, and freelancing, I'm also an ACE-certified personal trainer (and Les Mills BodyPump instructor!) and motivational speaker on topics ranging from healthful living to stress management to goal-setting. (Check out www.becomebodywise.com for more on the work I do.) I live outside Chicago with my husband, son, daughter, and maniac golden retriever, Sugar Cookie. I love ghostwriting and hope that you will, too.

Associations for Ghostwriters, Coauthors, and Authors

Want to be a more successful ghostwriter, coauthor, or author? Join the club…or rather, a like-minded organization. Here are three of interest to ghosts and coauthors:

American Society of Journalists and Authors

www.asja.org

ASJA consists of independent nonfiction writers (including ghosts and coauthors) who write magazine articles, books, and other forms of nonfiction writing. Membership benefits include confidential market and pay rate information, an exclusive freelance project referral service, seminars and workshops, and meetings with editors and agents. Dues: one-time initiation fee of $50; $210/year thereafter.

Association of Ghostwriters

www.associationofghostwriters.org

The Association of Ghostwriters includes ghostwriters of books, articles, speeches, blogs, and social media content. Its purpose is help members find ghostwriting assignments, develop and enhance writing and interviewing skills, deliver top-quality written materials, and manage profitable ghostwriting projects. Benefits include a ghostwriting job bank, monthly teleseminars and email newsletters, and discounted products and services. Dues: $99/year.

Authors Guild

http://authorsguild.org

The Authors Guild advocates for writers in matters like copyright protection, fair contracts, and free expression and includes authors, ghostwriters, and coauthors as members. The guild provides legal assistance and a broad range of web services to its members. First year dues are $90; after the first year, dues are charged on a sliding scale, depending on writing income, but most members continue to pay $90.

Made in the USA
Lexington, KY
04 May 2015